Box Lunch

Box Lunch

the layperson's guide to cunnilingus

Diana Cage

alyson books
los angeles

Manufactured in the United States of America.

This trade paperback original is published by Alyson Publications,
P.O. Box 4371, Los Angeles, California 90078-4371.
Distribution in the United Kingdom by Turnaround Publisher Services Ltd.,
Unit 3, Olympia Trading Estate, Coburg Road, Wood Green,
London N22 6TZ England.

First edition: July 2004

04 05 06 07 08 a 10 9 8 7 6 5 4 3 2 1

ISBN 1-55583-849-9

Library of Congress Cataloging-in-Publicaton Data
  Cage, Diana.
    Box lunch : a layperson's guide to cunilingus / Diana Cage. — 1st ed.
    ISBN 1-55583-849-9
    1. Sex instruction. 2. Oral sex. I. Title.
  HQ31.C224 2004
  613.9'6—DC22   2004043877

Credits
Cover illustration by Colleen Coover.
Cover design by Matt Sams.

Contents

Acknowledgments

Thanks to all the people that put up with me while I was writing this book. A special thanks goes to Ian Hendrie, who spent hours listening to me go on and on about oral sex and who gave me tips and tricks I could share with everyone. Thanks to Terri and Angela for coming up with the idea and overlooking deadlines. Thank you to Colleen Coover for the most amazing illustrations I've ever seen. You are wonderful. Thanks to Bridget Cannon for compiling the resource guide. Thank you to Adam and Tanya for giving me a place to live while I did research. I'm sorry about all the bloodstains on the sheets. Thanks to Blair for teaching me so much. Thanks to Shelley for keeping me from disappearing when I was in my hermit phase. Thanks to Bob Gluck for school help—without all the directed writings I would never have finished my M.F.A. Thanks to Tristan Taormino for teaching me so much at *On Our Backs*. Thanks to *On Our Backs* readers for keeping me challenged.

Introduction:
Confessions of a Cunnilingus Fiend

I love getting and giving head. It's really the one sex act I can't live without. There is nothing I'd rather do with my mouth—not even eat! And as far as my cunt is concerned...well, there may be lots of ways to get a woman to her happy place, but using your mouth is a sure way to make her really like you. Lick a lady into oblivion and she's going to keep you on her mailing list for a long time to come.

Cunnilingus is not a new thing. The act of kissing the genitals has been around as long as there has been kissing and genitals. *The Kama Sutra,* probably one of the best-known ancient (400 B.C.) love manuals of all time, has an entire chapter dedicated to giving women oral pleasure. With positions creatively named "The Quivering Kiss" and "The Circling Tongue," the guide makes it clear that oral congress was a highly developed act for ancient sex fiends.

Just about everything is great when you're getting busy with someone you really like. But really, nothing compares to the focused sensation of a hot wet tongue sliding over an erect clit. It's in a class all its own. And for scores of women—myself included—it's the fastest,

Cunnilingus Positions From The Kama Sutra

With delicate fingertips, pinch the arched lips of her house of love very very slowly together, and kiss them as though you kissed her lower lip: This is "Adhara-sphuritam" (The Quivering Kiss).

Now spread, indeed cleave asunder, that archway with your nose and let your tongue gently probe her "yoni" (vagina), with your nose, lips and chin slowly circling: it becomes "Jihva-bhramanaka" (The Circling Tongue).

Let your tongue rest for a moment in the archway to the flower-bowed Lord's temple before entering to worship vigorously, causing her seed to flow: This is "Jihva-mardita" (The Tongue Massage).

Next, fasten your lips to hers and take deep kisses from this lovely one, your beloved, nibbling at her and sucking hard at her clitoris: This is called "Chushita" (Sucked).

Cup, lift her young buttocks, let your tongue-tip probe her navel, slither down to rotate skilfully in the archway of the love-god's dwelling and lap her love-water: this is "Uchchushita" (Sucked Up).

Stirring the root of her thighs, which her own hands are gripping and holding widely apart, your fluted tongue drinks at her sacred spring: This is "Kshobhaka" (Stirring).

Place your darling on a couch, set her feet to your shoulders, clasp her waist, suck hard and let your tongue stir her overflowing love-temple: This is called "Bahuchushita" (Sucked Hard).

If the pair of you lie side by side, facing opposite ways, and kiss each other's secret parts using the fifteen techniques described above, it is known as "Kakila" (The Crow).

most direct route to that holiest of grails: the orgasm.

The first time someone went down on me I nearly died from pleasure. It was better than all my favorite things: watermelon, mangoes, a really great novel, trampolines, puppies, Camaros, vinyl hot pants, and sake all rolled into one. It was the most intense, exciting thing that had ever happened to me. My partner was

Many women claim that the orgasms they achieve through cunnilingus are stronger and more focused than those achieved through other means.

extremely talented and so eager that I felt like some kind of yummy dessert. She clearly knew her work. There was nothing nerve-racking or scary about the experience. It was all fun and sexy, and I was happy to lie back and enjoy myself. And the orgasm she gave me was so grand that I didn't want her to ever stop.

Sue may have blown *my* mind, but whether I could blow *hers* was another story. I was young and inexperienced and totally overwhelmed by my desire to please. Her pussy was a delight. It was beautiful and sexy, and I was thrilled to have my face pressed up against it. But let's face it, I didn't know what the hell I was doing. I was intimidated. I was in awe. I was standing at the edge of a gorgeous and totally new terrain. I fumbled around for a while, poking here and licking there and saying clumsy, uncool things like "Uh, is this OK?" until she got frustrated and flipped me and ate me out again. I'm lucky I was so eager to be a great lay, because that lesson could have turned me into a pillow queen of the worst kind.

Myth: The best way to get head all the time is
to be really bad at giving it.

Pussies are sensitive instruments. While most everything you can do to a vagina with your tongue is going to feel pretty good, it takes a certain amount of skill and technique to get her to grab your head, pull your hair, and scream "Don't stop, don't stop, I'm coming, I'm coming. Oh, God! I see God." My eager but unskilled tongue was just not up to the task. It's a good thing—no, a great thing—that Sue was willing and able to show me exactly how to please her. Otherwise I'd have ended up a pretty lousy lesbian.

Sue was very patient. She carefully told me what worked and what didn't, and taught me step-by-step how to blow her mind. She pulled her lips back and exposed herself to me, pointing out the extremely sensitive areas and the places where she preferred more pressure. And she did that all without ever making me feel clumsy or inexperienced.

Now, I've gone down on—and been gone down on by—many lovers since that time, but Sue pretty much gets the credit for making me into the rug-munching champ that I am today. And that's exactly why I wrote this book, so that every single one of you out there can pick it up and learn a thing or two about making your lady friend go crazy and scream your name. Being really great at going down is bound to make you popular. And the more popular you are, the more you'll get laid. And life is about getting laid, isn't it? Admit it, it is, or else you wouldn't be reading this.

Not that there's anything to be ashamed of if you're not already giving and getting great head. There are so many cultural taboos surrounding our pussies, it's no wonder people don't know what the hell they're doing down there. We worry, and our partners worry, that we smell bad or taste funny or that it will be unpleasant in some way. Our lovers worry that we aren't enjoying it or that they're going about it all wrong. We may even worry that our lovers will get bored because they aren't the ones receiving the pleasure. With all that worrying going on, how in the hell are we supposed to get off?

If you're a lesbian, you've got the burden of mastering what is generally considered to be the Ultimate Act of Lesbian Sex. And if you're a straight man, then you've got enough trouble without having to worry that your girlfriend is going to gossip about your lack of skill at polishing her pearl and make you the laughingstock of girls'-night-out banter and slumber party conversation. And let me tell you, sweetie, girls gossip. One ex-boyfriend of mine has been forever branded Big Mac Boy by my female friends because he ate pussy with so little finesse—it was like he was munching away on a meal deal.

One of the great things about licking box is that it can be as good for you as it is for her kitty. Your mouth gets to have a really good time. As much as eating pussy is physically enjoyable for the giver, it's also a very psychologically powerful turn-on. The woman splayed out in front of you is experiencing intense pleasure, and her entire body is reacting to the movements of your tongue.

Being good at going down is all about learning to love it. Confidence is key, and confident mistresses and masters of the oral arts are going to enjoy their time between her thighs as much as they enjoy anything she does between theirs. And confidence is exactly what the tips and techniques in this book are designed to give you.

Who Am I?

My main job, when I'm not thrilling women from coast to coast with my rug-munching prowess (just kidding), is being the editor of the world's only lesbian sex magazine, *On Our Backs*. Yes, I'm a professional lesbian! But I've had lovers of all genders, and this book is written for anyone who eats box—regardless of gender or sexual orientation.

As the editor of *On Our Backs,* I get to think about pussies—and what pleases them—all day, every day. I get to engage with readers, contributors, authors, video directors, and sex-toy makers who are interested in nothing but making pussies purr. Everyday I get letters from readers who have questions about oral sex. You'd be surprised at the number of lesbians out there who have trepidation about getting and giving head. And sadly it seems that many of us still think of giving head as something to do *to* our partners rather than *with* them. If there is one misconception I would like to change with this book, it's that cunnilingus is something that one person does *to* another. Cunnilingus is an act that two people do together. Just like any other sex act—except, of course, masturbating with the bathtub faucet.

The gist of many of my letters from women seems to be that they think no one really wants to go down on them—that anyone who does go down does it out of a sense of obligation—a "you do me, I'll do you" type of thing. But so many women and men I've spoken to say this isn't the case at all. Many, many eager beaver-lickers have told me that they—like me—think eating out is the best thing on earth. And hopefully, once you read this book, you'll agree.

And what about those nervous nellies out there who are afraid to get on their back—or knees or hands or rocking chairs or whatever? I know there are many of you who get so agitated at the thought of being prostrate before your love object that you can't come no matter how long someone licks you. Maybe being on your back feels too submissive because usually you're on top. Well, listen to me, babe. There are many ways to get done without giving up control. Climb on her face. Take charge. Or just try ordering your little pussy-licker around! Bottom-leaning lovers will go nuts when you command them to eat you out.

Just lie back and enjoy the ride...

No matter what your hang-up is, this book will help you relax and get into it. I'm going to make cunnilingus fun for the whole family.

In order to bring you as much useful information as I possibly could about cunnilingus I conducted a small but serious survey among as many lesbos, straight girls, transfolk, straight men, and other oral sex fiends of various genders that I could round up. I talked to them all about their worries, fears, loves, and hates about going south. And I learned a lot! Throughout the book I include tales related to me by that randy group of people. I think you'll find much of what they had to say enlightening.

For instance: One straight man explained to me that his main concern about going down on a woman that he wasn't seriously and romantically involved with was that it made him feel submissive and he didn't want to submit to a woman he didn't love! Well, straight men and lesbians may have a few things in common—and I'm not just talking about a love of box—but that sure as hell isn't one of them. For dykes, topping is all about giving pleasure. And the toppiest of the tops finds power in licking her lady's box and getting her to give up control. It just goes to show how power is all in the mind.

Another interesting little tidbit I learned was that some dykes don't actually like going down. Well, it's not like I *just* learned it—I knew that a few snatch-fearing dykes existed. But I had certainly never let any of them in my bed. I know you straight people think that lesbian loving is all about egalitarian sister-loving-sister vagina power. But that just isn't true. Just as many gay women as straight men have held onto their societally imposed misconceptions about the vagina being a dirty place. And some women are turned off by the smell and taste of their lovers' cunts. Well, if you're the lover of one of these reluctant rug-munchers, hopefully this book will help you enlighten the poor soul.

Why You Need This Book

Oral sex is plain old dirty fun. And if you're good at it, then you're sure to have a long and happy love life. Great sex is the key to happy relationships—hell, it's the key to happiness. Women can come harder, longer, and more often than men. And don't you want to be the one helping to make that happen? The female orgasm is a sight to behold. And having your face between her legs when it happens is just about the best box seat you can get.

If you've never helped a woman to ejaculate, then this book might just help you do that. Going down on a woman who squirts when she comes is a lot like going to Sea World and sitting in the first row of the Shamu show. You'll have fun at the show no matter where you sit, but getting splashed makes the experience that much more memorable. And it's a great story to tell your friends.

I'll also teach you about the subtle but mind-blowing pleasures of anilingus, also known as rimming. I'll give you hints and tips on shaving your kitty (or on shaving your girlfriend's). I even touch on some advanced techniques like clit-pumping and tell you which lubes least interfere with the taste of twat.

Want to make the world a better place? Start with becoming a better lover.

Happy licking!

One

A Guided Tour of the Pleasure Palace

A woman's genitals are as unique in appearance as her face. Twats come in so many shapes and sizes you can hardly recognize them from one to the next. While we've all got pretty much the same basic parts, the design on each model is totally different. It's important to know where all the roads lead if you want to get to your destination.

When was the last time you took a good long look at your cunt? Can you find your G spot? Do you know where your clitoral cruras are? Seriously. Even if you're a hoo-hoo master, I'll bet you can't name all the parts of the clitoris! (Hint: What we routinely call our clit is really just the tip of the iceberg.)

If you understand where everything is and what each part does, you'll have a greater mastery of your sexual response.

I'll always remember the first lover who got off on staring at my hoo-hoo. She had this weird habit of eating me out and then gazing in awe at my postorgasmic cunt. At first it totally freaked me out. She really stared hard, like an evil gynecologist plotting to impregnate me with alien babies. I had never withstood that type of scrutiny before, certainly not in broad daylight. I worried that it didn't look right. Maybe everyone else's

> The size and shape of female genitalia is rarely discussed in the locker room. No one ever says, "Damn, she had a huge cunt!" when reminiscing about his or her girlfriend.

was prettier. Was I too hairy? Not pink enough? Maybe I had an alien pussy. Maybe she was staring at it because it was so terrifying—like a train wreck. It wasn't until I went out of town for a week and she told me she'd been longingly visualizing my pussy the whole time and masturbating to the image that I began to feel excited. She told me she missed it so much, she drew pictures of it. Suddenly I felt like I had an exotic work of art down there.

Lesbians are at an advantage in the vaginal knowledge department because we see our lovers' pussies all the time. We get up close and personal with real cunts in all of their real imperfection. But most straight women don't have the kind of access to vaginas that you get from licking box all the time. Many of my straight female friends have told me that the majority of up-close-and-personal views they've had of various vulvas have come from porn. And worse than that, some women feel insecure about their own coochies when they don't look like the ones in *Playboy*.

Well, let me just set the record straight: Cunts don't really look like that. Trust me. I'm a pornographer.

The pussies you see in magazines like *Hustler* and *Playboy* have been pinkened and plucked and otherwise altered in Photoshop—an image-editing program used by graphic designers to digitally manipulate photographs. Not only are porn stars and *Playboy* models Photoshopped, but porn snatch starts out different from yours and mine to begin with. Those women make their living by having a pristine and childlike cha-cha. They spend lots and lots of money to get it perfect. They get Brazilian waxes. They get laser hair removal. They get laser vaginoplasty, or laser vaginal rejuvenation to make their cunts look pink and virginal all over. They also get labiaplasty—a process in which the labia are trimmed to specification. *Hello! They get their assholes bleached!* Porn cunts are totally engineered.

Your average cunt looks nothing like the private parts of a *Hustler* honey. We're all different. All gorgeous. And natural snatch is—like natural breasts—so much nicer than plastic.

"The first time I saw another woman's bare cunt was in my boyfriend's Penthouse magazine. The woman's inner lips were so tiny compared to mine, I thought for sure my pussy was ugly. My lips are long and uneven and stick out beyond my outer lips. I actually talked to my boyfriend about it, and he told me he thought my cunt was sexy. He said that the tiny, perfect pussies in the magazine weren't beautiful to him, and that in comparison my pussy looked juicy and fuckable."
—Jennifer

Let's start with a guided tour. If you own your own pussy, you can follow along at home with a hand mirror. If you don't have one of your own, feel free to use your lover's. If you don't have a girlfriend, go get a neighbor or something.

First stop on the pussy tour is the *mons,* or *mons veneris,* which is Latin for mound of Venus, also known as the *mons pubis* or just "the mound." It's the fleshy, comfy, cushy area between your legs where your bush grows. It's nicely padded to protect the pubic bone from impact during intercourse. It's a very sexually sensitive spot, and while it's not going to get anyone off, it's full of nerve endings, and lightly stroking your honey's mound before going below will fill her with shivers of delight.

Next we have the inner and outer labia. These are two sets of lips that surround all the sensitive insides. The outer lips, called the *labia majora,* are fleshy, padded, and hairy. The inner lips, or *labia minora,* are slippery little buggers that have no hair follicles. Inner lips come in every shade, from bright pink to burgundy to chocolate. They are extremely sensitive, often uneven in size, and sometimes long enough to extend past the outer lips. When a woman is aroused, the inner lips fill with blood, causing them to swell and turn darker. Many women love having their inner lips stimulated; some enjoy it more than direct stimulation of the clit.

Surgical Procedures Commonly Performed on the Vulvas of Porn Stars to Make Them Look "Perfect"

Laser reduction labioplasty: sculptures the elongated or unequal labia minora (small inner lips) according to one's specification

Laser perineoplasty: rejuvenates the relaxed or aging perineum; can also enhance the sagging labia majora (large outer lips) and labia minora to provide a more intact, tighter-looking vulva

Augmentation labioplasty: can provide aesthetically enhanced and youthful-looking labia majora by transplanting liposuctioned fat into the labia majora.

Whenever you see art in which the vagina is represented as an open blossom, the inner lips are the lucky parts that get portrayed as petals.

Other objects typically used to portray pussies:
shells • peaches • figs • almonds • oysters • mussels

Now we come to everyone's favorite magic bean, the *clitoris,* or *clit.* The clit is where a lot of the action happens. Think of it as similar to a penis, only with *four times* as many nerve endings. The part that most of us are referring to when we talk about our clits is actually just the head, or *glans,* of our clits. The clitoris is a complex organ that pretty much extends throughout the entire genital region. Anytime you make your lady feel good by stimulating her vagina, her butthole, her lips, or anywhere else down there, you're also indirectly stimulating her clit. The clitoris is the only organ in the human body—male or female—whose sole purpose is sexual pleasure.

The clitoris is a network of nerve-rich organs consisting of the *hood,* the *clitoral glans,* the *clitoral shaft,* the *crura* or legs of the clitoris, and the *clitoral bulbs.*

Until not too long ago, folks believed that the clit was just a little protruding button. But now, thanks to awesome books like Rebecca Chalker's *The Clitoral Truth* and *A New View of a Woman's Body* by the Federation of Feminist Women's Health Centers, we know it actually has many parts.

If you pull back the *hood* of the clit, you will expose the *glans* or visible nub of the clit—otherwise known as the little man (or woman) in the pink canoe. For clarity throughout this book, when we discuss the clit we are referring to this part of it.

The clit has about 8,000 nerve endings—more than any other structure in the human body. It's pretty much a different size and shape on every woman. If you're going down on a small-clitted gal, don't sweat it! Sensitivity doesn't correlate to size. No matter how big or small, they all do the same job. And figuring out how to get her off is just a matter of figuring out how she likes her bits fiddled. Big clits are showy and fun. I know a girl whose clit is so large, her lovers can jerk it off like a cock. Small, cute clits can be extra-sensitive, requiring light, feathery tongue licks—or not. Maybe she wants you to pound her bean like a jackhammer? You'll have to poke around and figure it out.

Pay close attention to the clit. It's going to be the focus of quite a bit of your oral effort. It's extremely sensitive, and stimulation of this baby is essential to most women's orgasms.

The clit is shrouded by the *clitoral hood,* a fold of draped tissue that keeps your sensitive nubbin safe from overstimulation.

The *shaft* of the clitoris runs just superior to the *clitoral glans.* Run your finger over the hood of the clit and press down on it. You should feel a rubbery cord extending up toward the bush. This cord could be anywhere from half an inch to an inch long. It's sensitive, and pressing on it should

75% of women require some sort of clitoral stimulation in order to reach orgasm.

feel good. Most women will find that massaging it gets them hot.

Before we get to the behind-the-scenes stuff, you should know that *vulva* is the term for all the parts you can see from the outside. That said, the *shaft* of the *clitoris* extends up toward the *mons,* then forks and bends around, forming two wishbone-shaped legs, or the *clitoral crura.* The *crura* run down either side of the vagina about three inches, below the surface, just behind the *labia minora.* The *crura* are too deep for you to feel with your fingers. But trust me, their presence is one reason penetration can feel so heavenly.

Starting from the point where the *shaft* and *crura* meet there are another two extensions—the *clitoral bulbs.* I told you this thing was big! The *clitoral bulbs* extend internally down and underneath each of the *labia minora.* They're bigger than the crura, and they fill with blood and get hard when a girl is all juiced up.

Below the clit you'll find the *urethral opening*—you know, your peehole. This is where urine leaves the body. It's also where ejaculate leaves the body. In both women and men the urethra is surrounded by a ring of spongy tissue that fills with fluid during arousal, and it's this fluid that comes squirting out during female ejaculation. What this fluid is made of is still up for debate, but everyone agrees that it isn't urine. The spongy tissue is called the *urethral sponge* or the *G spot.* It's pretty hard to locate if she's not yet turned on. But once she gets going, *Bam!* It's a big old hard button about the size of

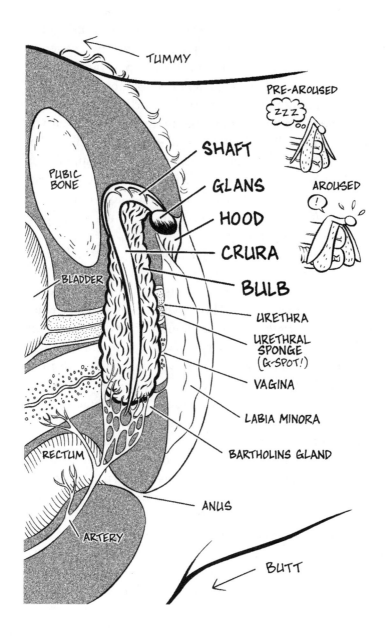

a quarter that you can push on and rock her world. You can feel the rough texture of the G spot if you stick two fingers in your honey's honey pot and prod around up toward the front wall of her pussy. That rough, textured, bumpy area is her G spot. Push on it, and she may feel like she has to pee. That's normal; you're poking around her urethra. Or maybe it will make her eyes roll back in her head—there's no telling. For many women, this is a huge erogenous zone, and stimulation of the G spot may make your girlfriend act like the Sparkletts Water Fantasy show at Sea World. You know that female ejaculation thing you've heard so much about? Well, this is where it all happens, baby.

Below the *urethra* is the *vaginal opening*. We think of the vagina as a tube, but really the walls of a woman's cooch lie flat against each other until she gets hot. The vaginal walls are a mucous membrane. This is why we get slippery when turned on; the walls exude the slippery stuff that makes sex so much fun. This slippery fun also helps to continuously flush out the whole works. The vagina is a self-cleaning organ. In other words, douching is *never* necessary. Douching is actually harmful. It fucks up the vagina's natural bacteria-killing acidic environment, leaving you open to possible infection. So if you're a woman and you've got some hang-ups about your smell and taste, the very worst thing you can do is douse yourself in chemicals. You're just going to create problems. And no one wants to eat a snatch that tastes like Bubblicious anyway.

When a woman gets all juiced up, the outer nerve-rich section of the vagina tightens up and gets hard, but the back two thirds of the sexual hallway—the less sensitive section— expands dramatically in length and width. This process is called *tenting*, and it's what makes vaginal fisting possible.

There's a lot more room in a pussy than you'd imagine.

Below the vaginal opening are two tiny little bean-sized glands called the *vulvovaginal glands* or the *Bartholins glands*. These babies don't do much except provide small amounts of lube during sex. They can get blocked and swell up, a painful and annoying event, but not life-threatening.

For most women reading this book, I'm guessing your *hymens* were obliterated long ago. But let's just pretend you've still got a cherry. It would be a thin membrane of tissue stretched across the opening of your hole. Most of the time this thing breaks before you ever get around to sticking anything up there. Just about any kind of strenuous activity can pop your cherry. But if you're kinky that way and you really want it back, you can have it surgically reconstructed.

The *cervix* is the opening to the *uterus*. If you stick your fingers up into the vagina you'll feel a round knob-like thing. It's a bit (doggy) nose-like. Yep, that's the cervix. It has an opening in the center called the *os*. This is the place from which menstrual blood escapes every month. The space inside the vagina on either side of the cervix is called the *fornix* and some women like this space explored with a finger, toy, or penis. While the cervix has no nerve endings on its surface, it responds to pressure. Bumping into it with a blunt object can feel good, or it can really hurt. Depends on the lady.

Since we're being thorough, I'll give you a quick run-down of the baby-making organs, though technically none of them figure into sexual arousal. But I wouldn't want to send you out into the world with only half of what you need to know about female sexual anatomy.

The *uterus* is where babies grow and where menstrual

cramps come from. It's about the size of a lemon. The *fallopian tubes* extend out and back from either side of the uterus. Each is a pathway from ovary to uterus, traveled by an egg from either the right or left *ovary* every month. The *ovaries* are located on either side of—and somewhat below—the *uterus*. They produce eggs and female sex hormones.

And that's about it.

Now Test Your Pussy Knowledge!

1. The vagina:
    a. has teeth
    b. should smell like grape Bubblicious
    c. "tents" during sexual arousal
2. The clitoris
    a. is just a cute little nubbin
    b. is actually an entire network of complex and nerve-rich organs
    c. is the way to a woman's heart
3. The G spot
    a. is a myth
    b . is a lesbian bar in Los Angeles
    c. might just make your lady go Boom!
4. The vulva
    a. is the name of the external female genitalia
    b. is a well-engineered Swedish car
    c. is often portrayed as a flower in feminist artwork
5. *Playboy* models' pussies look bright pink because
    a. pussies are supposed to look that way
    b. *Playboy* models are special
    c. they are Photoshopped beyond recognition

Fabulously Fun
Names to
Call Your Pussy

Alley
Altar of love
Angie
Apple
Artichoke
Ax wound
Banana split
Bank
Barge
Bazoo
Bearded clam
Bearded kitty
Bearded leisure center
Bearded oyster
Beaver
Beaver burger
Beehive
Bermuda Triangle
Biscuit
The bishop
Bit o' Honey
Bit of jam
Blind entrance

Blurt
Boat
Booty
Boris
Bottomless pit
Box
Breakfast of champions
Bull's-eye
Bun
Bun warmer
Buried treasure
Bush
Business
Butterfly
Buttonhole
Cabbage patch
Cake
Canal
Canyon
Carnal trap
Cat
Center of the universe
Chach

Cherry pie
Chimichanga
China
Choch
Chocha
Choo-choo
Christina Aguilera
Cigar box
Cockpit
Coin slot
Cooch
Coochie
Cookie
Cookie jar
Cooter
Cootie
Cooze
Crack
Crack of dawn
Creamsicle
Crevice
Critter
Crotch

Crown and feathers
Cum catcher
Cunnicle
Cunny
Cunt
Cupid's alley
The deep
Delicious
Divine scar
Dollhouse
Down there
Endless pit
Fajita
Fanny
Finest hour
Finger hole
Fish taco
Fishburger
Flesh blanket
Flesh wallet
Flowerpot
Fluffy
Flycatcher
Forest
Fruity fun
Fuck hole
Fun house
Fur trapper
Furburger
Furnace
Furry mongoose
Fury hoop
Fuzzy cup

The GAP
Garage
Gash
Gee
Gina
Ginch
Ginny
The goal
Golden doughnut
Good eatin'
Gopher hole
Grand Canyon
Grassy knoll
Gulf
Gully
Hair pie
Hairy whizzer
Hatch
Heaven
Heaven's gate
Her
Her highness
Her majesty
Hidden valley
Hirsute queen
Ho cake
Hole
Holiday Inn
Holster
Home
Home base
Home of the whopper
Home sweet home

Honey altar
Honey hole
Honeypot
Honey tree
Hoochie
Hoo-ha
Hoo-hoo
Hoop
Hot meat
Hot 'n' juicy
Hot Pocket
Jam pot
Jaws of life
Jelly roll
Juicy Lucy
Jungle
Keyhole
Kitty
Knish
Lady Jane
Lapland
Lily
Lips
Little Friend
Lollapalooza
Love box
Love button
Love highway
Love house
Love roller coaster
Love triangle
Lovers' Lane
Lucy

25

Lunch box
Mami
Map of Tasmania
Mink
Minnie Mouse
Money box
Monkey
Mossy swamp
Muff
Mystic rose
Nappy dugout
Nature's tufted treasure
Nest
Nether end
Nether lips
Nether mouth
Ocean
Ooze
Pandora's Box
Panocha
Peach
Pee-pee
Pencil grinder
Pie
Piece
Pink
Pink canoe
Pink eye
Pink palace in the black
Pirate's booty
Pirate's treasure
Pit
Playground

Playpen
Poon
Poondong
Poontang
Poox
Poozle
Portal of Venus
Punani
Puss
Pussy
Queen of the universe
Quic
Quicksand
Quiff
Quim
Red lane
Red Sea
Red snapper
Regina
Ripe peach
Ruby fruit
Rubyfruit Jungle
Salmon sandwich
Scabbard
Scented garden
Second hole from the back
   of the neck
See you next Tuesday
She
Sideways smile
Sister
Slant-eye
Slice

Slim
Slip 'n' Slide
Slipper
Slit
Snack cake
Snacky treat
Snapper
Snapping turtle
Snatch
South Pole
Split
Split loaf
Split peach
Squeeze box
Stench
Stephanie
Stinky Twinkie
Strange
Sugar
Sugar basin
Sugar doughnut
Sunny Delight
Sweet box
Sweet meat
Sweet piece
Sweet spot
Taco
Tail
Tang
Target
Teeny
Temple
Temple of Venus

Till Tuesday
Toolbox
Trench
Trim
Trout
Tube packer
Tuna pocket
Tuna sandwich
Tunnel
Tush

Twat
Vag
Vagina
Vaginal Davis
Velvet curtain
Velvet glove
Velvet Underground
Virginia
Vise pipe
Wallet

Wee-wot
Where the monkey sleeps
Whisker biscuit
White meat
Womanhood
Womb
Woo-woo
The Y
Yoni
Yum-yum

Two

Love Your Pussy

To really enjoy oral sex, you'll need to spend a little "me" time with your twat. Getting to know thyself is a great way to increase your orgasmic potential, get what you want out of sex, and make you better in the sack overall.

Masturbation is the key here. You've got to fiddle around with all the knobs and buttons to see which ones work best. Just pretend it's your lover's tongue doing all the work at the control panel.

If you're a slow come, then this self-love assignment is absolutely mandatory. Regular engine maintenance will increase your overall sex drive and heighten sexual responsiveness. And if you aren't a slow come, you should still jerk off. One of the great things about being a chick is multiple orgasms and no refractory period! Masturbating on a regular basis keeps you in touch with your sex drive. It keeps you sexually responsive and ready to go.

Not to get too New Agey, but I firmly believe that masturbation should be an event. Put the moves on yourself. Check out your hot bod in a full-length mirror. Flex your biceps. Do what you need to do to set the scene—light some candles, put on some lingerie or your sexiest boxers, turn on Ricki Lake, fondle your dildo collection, whatever gets you in the mood. But for this particular exercise, leave the Hitachi in the drawer. The goal here is to teach your cunt to respond to the slow, sensual tango of your partner's tongue. We're going to use some nicely lubed-up fingers as a substitute for the long pink muscle.

Before you start, take a minute or two to meditate on the thought that pussies rock and that yours rocks harder than anyone else's. Go get a hand mirror so you can watch yourself.

Even the most enlightened woman gets a little insecure from time to time about the smell, taste, or look of her special place. And there's nothing that will keep you from dialing O on the pink telephone like worrying that your lover is not enjoying his or her time between your thighs. So take a long look. Enjoy yourself. Notice how pretty everything is. Cup your entire vulva with your hand and feel the heat and pressure. Pull your lips apart. Lift back your clitoral hood and look at your magic bean. Say hi to your pussy!

Get out some lube. Later in the book we'll discuss which brands of lube affect your chach flavor the least, but for now anything water-based or silicone will do. No oils. You should know this by now, but oil-based anything is bad news for your vag. It can block up your pores and fuck up your delicate coochie ecosystem, leaving your vagina open to infection. Also, oils cling to the skin and are far more difficult to wash out. So stick with something nice and pussy-friendly like Probe or Liquid Silk.

Lube that baby up. Put a couple of drops on your fingertips and spread the love around. This is going to feel really great, so prepare to get turned on. Polish your pearl, pull on your labia, run a slippery digit all over your whole slit, maybe even stick some fingers in your hole. Do everything you'd like a tongue to do. Pay attention to what feels good. Get turned on. Talk dirty to yourself. Take note of what works. You will use this information later when you talk to your partner about things that turn you on. Remember: You should be watching the whole show in your hand mirror. Having both hands free will make this exploratory mission more enjoyable, so if you don't have a free-standing mirror, try propping it up against some pillows, or get creative with the ugly polka-dotted picture frame you got from your Aunt Beulah for your birthday. Notice things about the way your coochie looks throughout the different stages of arousal. Your inner lips will swell and darken. Your clit will get hard and poke its head out from under your clitoral hood. Everything will get redder and wetter. Your smell will become stronger and muskier. Turned-on twat is an excellent smell. Enjoy it. Revel in it.

You may or may not want to make yourself come during this little exploratory dive. Either way is good. The point of this exercise is to warm yourself up and really have a good time with your cunt. We want our lovers to enjoy the time they spend down there. So we need to take our own test drives once in a while just to see how smooth the ride is. This is also a great way to make sure all of your parts are in working order.

Love that thing between your legs. It brings you lots of pleasure. Appreciate it.

A Note for the Big, Bad Butch Girls

Femmes love to go down. They love your snatch. They want to eat you out as much as you want to eat them out. I know sometimes you may doubt that. Sometimes you wonder how to get off with your girl parts when you feel so masculine in the sack. Well, dude, let me put it this way: You like to lick box right? It's hot when you're using her thighs as earmuffs, and the noises she makes when she's about to go to her happy place are unbelievably sexy. You love her, and you want to make her happy. Her peach tastes like heaven, and there is nothing in the world better than a wet pussy on your face. Well, she feels the exact same way!

If you've bedded down with a confirmed pillow queen who wants nothing to do with getting you off, I say kick her out. If you're happy with that and prefer your O's self-administered—well, that's one thing. But if you want some face time and you aren't getting it, make yourself heard. Butches and femmes speak different languages. She may not know that you want her to go south. Be explicit about it. Communication is key. And if you're playing that game where you pretend like you don't want her to visit your down below but you secretly do, I don't know what to tell you. It takes a really tough girl to keep trying to get between a butch's thighs once she's been shot down. So give it up once in a while and tell her what you need. If you're normally on top, tell her in a really bossy voice. She'll love it.

The Scent of a Woman

How do you smell? How do you taste? Stick your fingers in your slipperiness and taste it. Mmm. Slightly tart? Tangy? Unless, of course, something is wrong, your taste should be pleasant and sexy. And your smell should be musky, heady, and sexy. Myths about fishy-smelling snatches have given a lot of us complexes. Not to mention all the commercials for Summer's Eve and Massengill and scented feminine hygiene products. Those things are awful! Not only that, they reek.

My friend Tanya once figured out that her boyfriend was cheating when she whiffed a box of "deodorant" mini pads in his bathroom. The smell was so strong she picked up on it when she went in to pee. When Tanya followed her nose to the cabinet under the sink, sure enough, there they were! She confronted him, and he confessed. He'd been two-timing, and girlfriend number 2 had stashed a few personal items in the bathroom. Consider yourself warned.

For the record, a healthy snapper does not smell bad. It smells awesome—like tangy, salty, slippery sex-fruit. If you're carrying around issues about the smell of your cooch, get over it. Healthy pussy smells heavenly. And anyone who doesn't think so is crazy and doesn't deserve to get snacky on your hair pie anyway.

Foods That May Make You Taste Good
pineapple • melon • kiwi fruit • strawberries • celery

Foods That May Make You Taste Bad
broccoli • meat • dairy products • asparagus • coffee • alcohol • cigarettes

The Most Fun I've Had Between a Pair of Thighs

The best head I've ever given was...wait, strike that—I can't say for sure I was her best. Though she told me so many times, postcoital pillow talk can't always be trusted. But I can truthfully tell you that she was my favorite person to please. It helped that I was head over heels in love and would have done just about anything to make her happy. She was a gorgeous girl. A blue-eyed, tomboyish dyke with soft skin and faggy sensibilities and a healthy love of sex. But the main reason she was so fun to go down on was that she loved it. She got into it with a delight unmatched by any other woman I've had the pleasure of orally adoring. She'd grab my head and pull my hair and grind her crotch against my mouth. She'd moan and groan and call my name. Her pussy was so responsive that I could make her come in minutes, though I loved to draw it out and make her wait. And when she got close to coming she'd hold my head with such force that several times she cut off my air supply. I would lick away with glee just hoping she'd reach orgasm before I fainted.

What made going down on her so great was her sheer pleasure as lickee and her total lack of self-consciousness about her cunt. She had an attitude about her cunt that I've not come across again. She knew it was delightful. And she knew I'd enjoy it. And that, I'm telling you, was incredibly hot.

Keeping It Clean

OK, just because I keep telling you how nasty and disgusting scented feminine hygiene products are doesn't mean you shouldn't wash! We all want to be clean for our lovers. Keeping clean and well-groomed is an essential part of being sexy and desirable. I don't care if you're butch or femme or what, you want your love box to be a scented garden of delight that lovers trip over themselves in a rush to get to. And while au naturel cunt is pretty great, cleanliness is next to goddessliness—or something like that.

Here's a little-known fact: Deodorant soaps are not great for the vagina. While they probably won't kill you, their alkaline nature disturbs the naturally acidic environment of your puss, the pH of which hovers somewhere around a tangy 5, or about the same as a glass of wine. This acidic environment helps to prevent the growth of bacteria. Upset the balance and you ruin the vaginal ecosystem, leaving the cooch host to all sorts of unwelcome visitors. A low-pH soap without a lot of harsh chemicals will treat your box right. Castile soaps, like Dr. Bronner's, have a mildly acidic pH and will get you all clean and nice without washing away your natural protective barrier. Try Dr. Bronner's peppermint if you want a little thrill!

Nervous about your partner's taste and smell? Try taking a shower together beforehand. You can have naughty foreplay fun in the shower and make sure your lady is fresh and clean at the same time.

Menstruation

If she feels sexy during her period and the two of you are fluid-bonded (meaning you've been tested for STDs and agreed to share bodily fluids with each other; you must use safe sex precautions with all other partners and be in complete agreement about the risks you are taking), then there's no reason not to head south when she's menstruating. If menstrual blood is a turnoff for you, she can wear a tampon or use the Instead Cup, a rubber cup that fits over the cervix, forming a seal. It keeps any blood safely inside. The Instead Cup can be tricky the first few times you use it, so take a test run before the real deal.

Another option is to use dams or Saran Wrap to keep blood at bay. Whether or not to go down while she's bleeding is totally up to the two of you.

Some people actually find the smell and taste of menstrual blood to be a turn-on. More power to them. Just remember the presence of blood increases the chance of transmitting disease.

"I really like going down on my wife when she is on her period. She gets really turned on when she's bleeding. And I like the musky odor of her pussy. We usually just put a towel down on the bed and go to town. I've never really understood why some people get so hung up about it."
—Charlie

How to Shave for Sex

Let's talk pubes. A shaved vulva has some perks, but many people enjoy the ambiance of a full, lush bush. Sexy is subjective. It's important to respect a woman's right to choose.

In the end, the decision of whether or not you should shave comes completely down to you. I have had lovers who kept their whole kitty completely bare, and I loved the feel of my tongue against their smooth, slippery folds. Not to mention the sight of their naked love boxes. A shaved snatch is more than just bare, it's naked. Hair hides everything. Without hair, all of your secret inner bits are right out in the open.

But I've also had lovers with bush that looked like Pam Grier's Afro in *Foxy Brown*. We're talking bush so big it goes *whoosh* when you unleash it from her 501's. Seventies bush. And it's incredibly sexy on a woman who feels comfortable in her skin.

I have no preferences when it comes to pubes. Whether a woman is bare or busy, if she's happy, I'm happy.

That said, there are a few advantages to shaving, the main one being a higher tongue-to-skin ratio. And let me tell you, if you're normally a fuzzy sort, presenting your lover with naked pink is a great way to mix it up. Variety is the spice of a great sex life.

If you're not into shaving but want to make your sweetie's time between your thighs more comfortable, you can trim the pubes along the base of your mons—the section at the top of labia that shrouds the clit. It won't drastically alter the look of your bush, but it will make for fewer hairs getting caught between your lover's tongue and your love button and generally make getting to your sensitive parts a little more convenient to

"Sex when I'm freshly shaved is the best. I really like the way my bare vulva looks." —Laurie

reach. Use small scissors to trim. Long ones are too unwieldy, and you don't want to accidentally snip something off!

If you're ready to make that leap to naked puss, there are a few rules to follow. Shaving takes some prep work, or else you risk ingrown hairs and razor burn. Also, it may itch as it grows back, so keep that in mind if you aren't ready to do the weekly upkeep. After you've shaved a few times, it's not so bad. Your skin adjusts to the feel, and everything is less sensitive. But the first time you shave you'll find that the itching of stubbly pubes growing back will drive you crazy.

And one more thing, though I shouldn't have to say this: If you're shaving your lover's puss as a form of sex play or because you're her lifestyle submissive or just because it gets you hot, be sure you haven't consumed any intoxicating substances. If you can't operate heavy machinery, you shouldn't go near someone's tender bits with sharp objects. Shaving is serious stuff.

The Perks of Shaving

Nothing says ready for sex like a bare vulva. Picture a woman's newly shaven, glistening wet cunt, the lips bare and parted, her swollen clit exposed. Hot, isn't it? Of course it is. And that's exactly why you would want to get rid of all that stubborn pubic hair, so you can see what's behind it. Nothing feels softer or more velvety to your fingertips than a newly shorn pussy. As an added bonus, you'll get to see more of the action while fucking. Removing the hair from your vulva is like undressing it. Take your kitty (or your lover's) from schoolgirl to call girl in a few easy steps.

Gather Your Tools

You will need a razor, hair conditioner, shaving cream, and a hand mirror. For a razor, I personally swear by the Gillette Mach 3 and won't go near my crotch with anything else. However, many women tell me disposable razors work very well and actually help to prevent ingrown hairs— ostensibly because they don't cut the hair as close to the skin as a triple-blade razor. Go with what feels right to you.

Trim

If your pubes are long and shaggy, you'll need to trim them down to a manageable length before you shave them off. Beard clippers work very well, but small scissors are easier to maneuver. Trim as close to the skin as you can safely manage. Be careful down there! My friend Angela has a notch on her left labia from being a little clumsy with the scissors.

Take a Bath

A nice hot bath will prep you for a comfortable shaving experience. You want the hair to be as soft as possible before you try to remove it. This is an important step. Women who've shaved once without heeding this advice remain forever convinced that there is no way to go bare without a lot of itching and irritation. But they're wrong. And they're forever doomed to miss out on the pleasure of naked pussy lips against a nice wet tongue.

Make the experience erotic. If you'll be shaving your lover, why not join her in the tub? Wash her cunt gently and apply conditioner to her pubic hair. Let it soak in while you gently wash and fondle the rest of her. Get her in the mood. If this is your bush's first introduction to a razor, soak for at least 20 minutes.

Wash 'n' Go.

So you've soaked for a sufficient amount of time. You've applied conditioner to your pubes and let it sit for a minute or two. You're all rinsed and ready to go. Now comes the tricky part. Prop your butt on the edge of the tub and grab your razor. Lather up with shaving cream and decide what you'll be taking off and what you'll be leaving behind. A fully bare mons might look too prepubescent. You have the option of shaving the lips and leaving a bit of a beard on top. Perhaps you want a landing strip, or you want the whole thing naked. Make up your mind about where to begin and make few strokes *in the direction of the hair growth*. Rinse the razor in warm water after each swipe. The idea is to do this in as few strokes as possible to help avoid irritation. Try not to go over the same area repeatedly.

The Nitty-Gritty

Your cunt has a lot of nooks and crannies and crevices that can be difficult to reach. In order to get a smooth shave on the inner bits of your outer labia, stretch them taut with your hand. For your *perineum* (the area between your vagina and anus) you'll want to squat in the bathtub and check out the area with a hand mirror. Prop the mirror up in the tub so both hands are free. You can guide the blade easily by feeling around down there with your free hand—you don't need to watch every stroke in the mirror. But having a mirror handy will keep you from accidentally leaving any furry spots. Make sure to *carefully* shave around your asshole for a totally smooth experience.

Dare to Be Bare

When you've finished, rinse off the shaving cream and pat dry with a towel. Find something suitably crotchless or see-through to show off your new do. Or simply flaunt it naked for your lover. Make sure to enjoy all the new sensations you'll experience. Notice how soft and smooth you are. Notice how nice lube feels against your naked skin. Your lover's tongue now has a whole new terrain to cover.

Mind the Beard

Beard burn can be a nasty thing. And if you're part of a het couple or your lover is either on testosterone or naturally hirsute, then you will have to deal with beard. A bare vulva is very sensitive, and if you're a hairy-faced type, you will want to be clean-shaven to avoid pricking all her sensitive parts with tiny, sharp hairs. You may not realize it if she hasn't said anything, but beard burn hurts *a lot.*

For women who shave, this also works the other way around. Your lover's face is going to be all snuggled up against your mound. If you haven't shaved in a day or so and the area has become a stubble danger zone, you should be aware that the prickly hairs around the top of the outer

Fun Shapes, Anyone?

Shaving your pubes into the shape of a heart or a star is a sexy surprise for anyone who ends up in your pants. It's a little tricky without a stencil to follow, so first cut your desired shape out of some cardboard. Hold the stencil against your wet and lightly lathered mound and carefully shave around it. If you really want to please your sweetie, carve his or her initials down there!

lips can wreak havoc on a sensitive face. Staying clean-shaven is best, but if you don't have time for that, holding the outer lips apart with your fingers as you lovers eats you out will keep her or his face from getting all rashy and sore.

Saving Face

One way to avoid pussy-inflicted beard burn is to use some form of depilatory or wax.

Waxing is an option many people swear by. It lasts much longer than shaving, but it's a lot more involved and somewhat painful (though not really that bad, and you quickly grow used to it).

If you just want to clean up the hairs around your bikini line, then you can probably handle waxing at home with any of the kits available at the drugstore. But if you're looking to go totally bare, you'll need a Brazilian. A Brazilian is a very thorough wax job in which *everything* is waxed. It's the difference between taking your car in for auto detailing rather than driving it through the free wash you get with a fill-up. It's not just the mons that gets cleaned up, but the entire outer labia, perineum, ass crack, and anus. It's not for the shy. The person administering the wax will ask you to hold your legs very far apart. In fact, she may even ask you to hold your legs up by putting your hands behind your knees. You might also have to get down on all fours so that she can have access to the hair around your anus. Yeah, it's a pretty vulnerable-feeling position, to say the least.

The aesthetician is going to spread hot wax all over your private parts, press a piece of fabric against the hot wax, and quickly rip it off against the direction of the hair growth. Then she'll come in for the kill with a pair of tweezers to pluck any remaining strays. You and your aesthetician are going to be very close at this point. It's not fun, but the pain subsides quickly, and after you've done it a few times, it really doesn't seem so bad. The best part: The results last about four weeks.

Some women prefer depilatory creams or liquids that

dissolve the hair below the surface of the skin. I have never found any to work very well, but porn star and registered nurse Nina Hartley once recommended a product called Magic Shave in the pages of *On Our Backs* (October-November 2002). Several readers immediately wrote in to the magazine claiming that Magic Shave changed their lives, freed them from ingrown hair hell, whitened their teeth, and did all sorts of other magical things. So if you don't like razors or hot wax, you may want to give it a try. It's available at the drugstore, probably in the African-American hair care section. The product is designed for men who have trouble with shaving and razor bumps due to the curly nature of their beards.

Three

Getting in the Mood

When a lady gets turned on, all sorts of cool things happen to her coochie. First the brain begins the turn-on process by receiving sexually arousing stimuli from the body. This stimuli could be getting a peek at her girlfriend naked. It could be that she's getting her nips pinched; it could be that she's watching a really good episode of the new *Fantasy Island*. Whatever it is, the first two changes that take place are called vasocongestion and mytonia.

Vasocongestion is a pooling of the blood in the hot zones, namely the breasts and the crotch. This pooling of blood causes those regions to swell: Breasts grow heavier, pussy lips plump up, your clit hardens. It also causes these regions of the body to feel warm to the touch and darken in color, and it gets the pussy wet by forcing moisture to seep out through the vaginal walls.

The clitoral glans grows and pokes out from under its little turtleneck, the hood. The clitoral legs stiffen and grow larger and longer, pushing out the inner and outer labia and making the entire vulva puffy and swollen. The clitoral shaft grows longer and hardens, and you're able to feel it with your finger—try rolling your fingertip back and forth across it. It feels like a cord or a straw. At this point the uterus and cervix pull up and the inner two thirds of the vagina expands.

When a woman is turned on her skin becomes supersensitive. Her heart rate increases, and her blood pressure goes up. She's shooting off a potent cocktail of sex chemicals, and these chemicals are making her entire body scream, "More! More!"

Her pussy is probably pretty wet by this time, though the amount of wetness varies from woman to woman and is affected by where a woman is in her menstrual cycle. Some pussies soak the bed; some don't. It's all normal.

Remember that a woman's juiciness is not a reliable indicator of readiness for sex. A totally wet snatch might just be getting started, and a bone-dry one might be dying to get off. In a fully aroused cunt, the vulva is open and swollen and the vaginal opening is exposed. Keep that in mind next time you're about to stick something in one.

Facts About the Clitoris

- Women get "clitters" (clitoral hard-ons) every 90 minutes during sleep.
- An aroused clit doubles in size.
- On average, it takes 15 seconds for a clit to return to its normal size after orgasm.

As your lady gets hotter, she will start to feel a yummy muscular tension in her pelvic region. This tension is the mytonia that we mentioned earlier, and it will continue to build as she gets more and more turned on, eventually releasing in the most delightful way during a few seconds of blissful muscle contraction, that holiest of holies, the orgasm.

According to Masters and Johnson, the longest orgasm ever recorded is 43 seconds. But if you've seen Annie Sprinkle's excellent video *Sluts and Goddesses,* you know that's a crock because the Sprinkle herself has one that lasts for five full minutes. *Aw, yeah.*

For chicks, orgasms are like pistachios—you can just keep having them, one after the other after the other. Not only that, but we come harder and longer than guys do. God must love us.

Oral Sex *Is* Sex

One of the main misconceptions about oral sex is that it's a precursor to the main event—penetration. Well, let me set the record straight. Licking your gal's coochie can certainly be a great way to warm her up for intercourse, but oral sex is more than foreplay. Oral sex is a *main event.* That's why you're reading a book about it. Forget fucking! Sure, fucking is great. But straight-up fucking just doesn't do it for most women the way a tongue bath does. Cunnilingus is the most reliable way to dial O on the pink telephone.

She should be turned on before you go anywhere near her nether region with your tongue. The clit needs time to adjust, her hormones need to get flowing, and her genitals need to become engorged before they're able to transmit all the pleasurable sensations you're about to deliver. Whatever you do, do not go stampeding to the clit. If your woman isn't hot and bothered, her little nubbin will either be totally insensitive or way oversensitive—and neither state is a nice one.

Oral sex is not foreplay. Oral sex requires foreplay. Lots of it. Before you go down on her, get her ready.

Turn Her On

So how do you get your lady friend to this wonderful state called *really turned on*? You want her to beg for your tongue. You want her to want it *bad*. But what do you do to get her there? Well, grasshopper, the truth is, it varies from chick to chick. And it takes more than a Luther Vandross album and a red lightbulb. Yes, that's right. You're going to have to learn to communicate.

Talking with your partner about sex can be a turn-on in and of itself. A simple game of "tell me what you like" can get her talking dirty and visualizing all sorts of scenarios. When it's your turn, tell her quietly—maybe whisper in her ear—all the ways in which you plan to pleasure her. Watch her reactions carefully. Does her chest rise and fall more rapidly as her breathing accelerates? Does her face flush? Does she squirm? Look away? Does she clutch at you and start humping the bed? (That's always a good sign.)

How to Talk Dirty to Your Lover

Make lots of noise. When something feels good, moan appreciatively. Gasp, sigh, breathe loudly, whimper. Make noises that show you care. Making noise heightens your partner's pleasure as well as your own and provides feedback so he or she knows what a good job they're doing. A couple of well-timed "Oh, yes, Oh, yes" sighs can take you far.

Practice makes perfect. If saying the word "cunt" out loud makes you blush, try practicing while you jerk off. Say dirty words out loud while you touch yourself. Describe what's happening as you're doing it. "I'm fingering my cunt." "My pussy is so wet."

Test-drive your new skills on the phone. Feeling shy? Test-drive your dirty talk during phone sex. It's easier because your honey can't see you blush. You get some semblance of privacy, and you can play it cool even when you're cringing inside.

Narrate the story. Talk to your partner about what you are doing to her as you are doing it. "Baby, I'm fucking you so hard right now." This works better during activities other than oral sex, because it's not polite to talk with your mouth full.

Make her feel sexy. Things like "Your body turns me on" and "I love to look at you naked" are surefire winners. Tell her she's beautiful. Talk about her cunt. Describe how wet it is, how swollen her clit is, how much you'd like to put your mouth on it. Every time my partner says, "Mmm, wet pussy," I melt. Try it.

Ask questions. Dirty questions are a no-brainer way to get some dirty talk flowing. Try "Do you want my mouth on your clit?" "Should I suck you harder?" or "Tell me what you think about when you masturbate."

Get her to talk about how it feels. "How does this feel?" works very well. And you can always be more specific with pointed questions, like "How does my tongue feel on your asshole?"

Use terms you're both comfortable with. Don't try and go from 0 to 60 without warming up. If your partner usually says "down there" when referring to her puss, then stick with that for a while until dirty talk gets easier for both of you. "Let me lick you down there, baby," is still very sexy. Suddenly yelling, "Rip me open with your hot throbbing rod!" is either going to cause her to laugh or cry.

Bark orders! "Get down on your knees!" "Bend over!" "Grab your ankles!" "Fuck me, you dirty whore!" Orders like these are sure to have a positive effect.

Sound confident. Lower your voice. Say dirty things with confidence if you want your partner to believe you. Fake it if you must, but try not to sound embarrassed. You can get away with just about anything as long as you own it. And whatever you do, don't giggle!

To get her thinking about sex during the day, whisper naughty things into her ear before she leaves for work. In this digital age, flirting via e-mail is fun and easy. And it's much more interesting than actually working. E-mail her dirty little notes listing all the things you're going to do to her when she gets home. But only if her e-mail is private. Beware her company's spam filters! They could get you caught if they're designed to search for dirty words. You may want to make up pet names for her muffin. *Pussy* is a surefire spam hit. When in doubt, don't risk it—unless you want the entire IT department at your girlfriend's company to know the intimate details of your sex life.

Lovers who talk openly about sex with each other stand a higher chance of keeping each other happy in the bed department and will have a longer and more satisfying love life.

Leave her voice-mail messages telling her you think about her and her gorgeous pussy. Before she leaves for work in the morning, tell her you're dying to get it on with her that night. Or better yet, start fooling around with her, lick her, touch her, tease her. Then send her off to work and make her wait a full eight-hour day for the grand finale.

Kiss her. A lot. Even more than that. Kissing is the most perfect sex act ever invented, and it's the perfect way to give her a hint as to what your tongue can do.

Play with her breasts! Breasts are sensitive little bundles of love. Caress them, worship them, adore them, and she will be grateful.

Play Nice With Her Tits

The prevalence of big-titted bimbos in mainstream porn has led many a lesbian to believe that breast obsessions are decidedly hetero. But I'm here to tell you that's not true. Lesbians like tits too! I've got a thing for boobs, and I'm not ashamed to admit it.Big or small or in between, they're supercharged erogenous zones. Nipples can be extremely sensitive, and in many women there is a direct, almost electric, connection between the nipples and the clit. I know women who can orgasm from nipple play alone, and if that isn't a reason to explore serious breast play, then I can't imagine what is.

Warm Her Up

Want her to shudder at your every touch? Start lightly. Gently stroke the sides of her breasts with your fingertips and the palm of your hand. Touch her softly, tease her through her clothes, until she starts to ache for more. Don't rip her bra off right away! She probably spent loads of money on that thing. Appreciate it. Tease and tickle and nibble her through her bra. Wait until she's actually pressing herself against your hands before you give her the stronger sensation she's craving. For the strokee: Entice her. Find out what she likes to look at. Wear revealing tops. Busty? Push-up bras are good. Corsets are even better. Small breasts look great braless, especially beneath tight white T-shirts.

Nipples Are for Sucking

Nipples feel fantastic between your lips and under your tongue. Wet her erect nipples with your mouth before blowing cool air on them. Nibble and suck them, but first gauge her pain tolerance. If she says "harder, harder," you can bet you're doing it right. If her breasts are large, she might be able to suck her own nipples. Ask her to perform for you.

Different Strokes

Try out different types of sensation on her until you find something that drives her wild. Rub an erect nipple with ice, then wrap your warm lips around it. Different temperatures will elicit different responses. You can bite them hard or nuzzle them softly. Squeeze her breasts firmly with your hands. Pinch her nipples, gradually increasing the intensity. Try brushing them with different textures. Hard, scratchy things are exquisite torture. Soft, fuzzy things will make her purr. Here, kitty!

Clamp Down

Nipple clamps, clothespins, barrettes, and other pinchy things can be used to keep the nipple stimulation going while your hands and mouth are busy elsewhere. If the clamps have a chain connecting them, pull it while you lick her pussy. Or have her keep it in her mouth like a bridle while you fuck her. Keep in mind, though, that clamps restrict blood flow to the tissue. Once the initial shock of pain subsides, she'll feel a dull ache. But the pain comes back— hard—when you remove the clamps and blood flows rapidly back into the area. Don't leave them on for too long; they can damage tissue. Twenty to 30 minutes maximum is a good rule.

Piercings Are Fun

Piercings are more than just decoration. Many people find that nipple piercings make their nips more sensitive. Try tugging the rings or barbells with your teeth or rolling them around in your mouth. Always make sure a piercing is completely healed before you play with it.

Titty Fucking

Seeing your cock buried between a woman's soft breasts is a visual thrill that can't be beat. Lube up your cock or dildo and her chest with something nonsticky. Hand lotion and silicone lube work well. Water-based lube will dry too quickly. If she's tall enough, have her kneel in front of you and push her breasts together. Then slide your cock between them, back and forth. Build up a good rhythm—really let yourself go. For the fuckee: That big rod sliding back and forth between your boobs feels pretty good, doesn't it? I bet you've never felt so objectified before. Isn't it hot?

The Butch Body

Some butch women feel ambivalent toward their breasts. Perhaps they never learned to eroticize them or they feel uncomfortable with the idea of tit play because breasts are seen as girly parts. Breasts can be an outward indication of a femininity that butch dykes don't feel inwardly in touch with. If this is the case, remind her that boys have nipples too and there is nothing specifically feminine about enjoying them. Gay men love to have their tits tugged and worked. The butchest of hard-core leathermen knows all about the pleasures of tit play. Try referring to her breasts as her pecs and treat her like a fag. You could open up a whole new erogenous zone for her.

Teach Your Partner to Love Going South

I once had an orally reluctant girlfriend. I had an orally reluctant boyfriend more than once. I know I've got a little lesbian prejudice going, but I've run across a lot more guys than girls who were reluctant to polish my pearl. So how do you put the oral special on the menu if you're getting offered the prix fixe? If your partner won't go down, it's a totally fixable situation.

First of all, talk to your partner. Make oral sex hot for him or her. Confess your cunnilingus fantasies. Tell your partner how excited the idea of her or his face between your thighs gets you. Chances are that what you're dealing with is performance anxiety. I'd be willing to put money on the fact that she or he is more worried that they won't please you than that they won't like it. By communicating openly with your would-be licker you can help allay his or her fears. Give your lover positive feedback about his or her oral skills and don't be shy about giving direction. Keep it sexy; don't get all Mack Daddy on her ass and start bossing her around, but a little bit of "Baby, that feels so-o-o good, could you lick me harder? Oh yes, right there, that's the spot!" will go a long way toward making her more confident while she's down there.

"I love going down on girls. I could eat pussy for hours. I especially enjoy it when a woman is really comfortable with her body. The girl I'm dating squeezes my head between her thighs and pulls my hair hard when she comes. It's superhot. She's a tall, athletic girl, really sexy, and really comfortable with receiving oral sex. The best time was just recently when we did it in her office. She teaches English composition to undergraduates at the university I attend. I showed up during her office hours and went down on her. She was sitting in her office chair, and I was in front of her on my knees. She had her pants down around her ankles and my head between her legs. I was glad no students came in for advising!"

—Renee

If your sweetie really has a distaste for oral sex, then a little bit of education mixed with titillation might help ease some of his or her anxieties. There are several great educational videos out there. And sexy videos have the added benefit of placing the act of rug-munching in an erotic context. Your lover gets to learn about oral sex techniques while watching people enjoy performing and receiving. *Nina Hartley's Guide to Cunnilingus* is a great video to start with. Any porn video with good oral sex scenes can also help to eroticize pussy eating. It's important to note, however, that most mainstream pornos are a terrible place to learn technique. Half the time the performers are doing a lot of silly moves that look good for the camera but don't actually feel good. There are exceptions, though, and watching porn together can be a great tool for couples looking to improve their sex life. I'm a fan of any video by the dyke porn company S.I.R. Video. They contain realistic depictions of lesbian sex, with hot, horny performers and real butches (yum!). Also, the *No Man's Land* series is

a mainstream all-female porn series that actually depicts authentic, hot-as-hell box-licking.

Another way to encourage your lover to engage in new types of sex play is to read aloud to him or her from your favorite smutty book. Lesbian erotica collections are a great place to find hot oral sex scenes. *Best Lesbian Erotica* is a series edited by sex educator and porn star-director Tristan Taormino. Also, *On Our Backs: The Best Erotic Fiction* and *On Our Backs: The Best Erotic Fiction 2* are good sources for hot lesbian licking stories. Check the resource guide at the back of this book for other suggestions.

Never force a lover to do something s/he doesn't want to do. Coercing a partner into sex will only create unhealthy resentment. Whining, bitching, and complaining aren't sexy. They won't get you laid—and they'll probably ruin your relationship.

Four

Getting Down to Business

Mind-blowing, head-grabbing, bed-rocking oral sex means different things to different women. One gal might prefer to have her labia delicately nibbled, and maybe the next one wants you to handcuff her and finger her asshole while you suck her clit like a cock. It pays to experiment with different techniques until you discover the perfect way to set your lady's crotch on fire. Keep in mind, though, that just because you've found the right tongue strokes on Tuesday night doesn't mean the formula will rock her world on Saturday. Being flexible and willing to go with the flow is the key to being a great tongue artist.

Start Slowly

Listen, buddy, you can't make a woman come faster by skipping the foreplay. In fact, you'll just slow down the whole process.

If you don't want to risk a neck injury, don't go rushing ahead to the clit—slow and steady wins the race. I can't tell you how many times I've had a lover dive in and start munching away without properly warming me up. When I was younger, I was often too shy to talk about sex with my

Other Names for Cunnilingus

Blowing some tunes
Box lunch
Canyon yodeling
Carpet munching
Clam diving
Clam lapping
Cunt lapping
Dining at the Y
Drinking at the fuzzy cup
Eating a tuna sandwich
Eating hair pie
Eating out
Eating pussy
Eating seafood
Egg McMuff
Face job

Giving head
Going south
Grinning in the canyon
Growling at the badger
Impersonating Stalin
Lapping cunt
Muff diving
Mumbling in the moss
Rug munching
Sipping at the fuzzy cup
Sitting on your face
Skin diving
Talking to the canoe driver
Tongue fucking
Whistling in the weeds
Yodeling up the valley

lovers, and my poor partner would end up spending the better part of an hour wearing my thighs as earmuffs. Get your gal ready with your fingers, lips, tongue, voice, etc.

40% of women will reach orgasm after 10 minutes of clitoral stimulation.

Plan on being down there a while and get comfortable. There are lots of positions in which to experience the wonders of oral activity, but if she's lying on her back and your face is between her legs, you're off to a good start.

She might need a pillow behind her back so that she can sit up and watch your tongue as it works its way across her vulva. In fact, one of the hotter oral sessions I've ever had involved me sitting up on the couch and my partner crouching between my legs. I had such a great angle on her tongue that I nearly came from the visual alone. To prevent neck kinks, it might also help to elevate her hips with a pillow.

90% of women will reach orgasm after 20 minutes of clitoral stimulation

Start out with indirect stimulation. Lightly kiss her clit above the hood, lick the inside of her thighs, nibble her outer labia and perineum. Lick everywhere you can without actually coming into contact with her hard little button. Talk to her. Use your sexy, whispery, deep sex-voice. Call her "sugar," "baby," "Daddy," or whatever she responds to. Use your imagination. Bring everything into play. You have more tools at your disposal than just your tongue. You can use your teeth—gentle nibbles feel wonderful. Try lightly rubbing your teeth along the shaft of her clit or lightly nipping at her outer labia. You can use your lips too: Try rubbing them against her slippery inner labes or grabbing her clit between them. You can breathe on her, blow on her (but never into her), hum a tune against her mound (but pick a tune that won't make her laugh—"Row, Row, Row Your Boat" is too silly). Be creative. Run a fingertip across her asshole or rim her lightly with your tongue. If you've never rimmed anyone before, turn to Chapter 9 for tips on pleasuring this sensitive little spot.

Anal play is the way to many a woman's heart.

It's a good idea to incorporate the rest of her body as well. The longer the warm-up process, the more she'll enjoy the main event. Touch her breasts, suck her nipples, and lightly bite them. Stroke her ass, hips, and legs. Suck her toes! Toes are totally underrated erogenous zones. In fact, as a lickee, it's a good idea to always be nook-and-cranny-prepared. Don't forget about your feet. Good grooming always pays off. So pedicure those puppies! (See page 58 for tips.) You never know which new lover might turn out to have a tootsie fetish.

As she gets hotter, you'll probably find that she craves stronger stimulation. Pay close attention. She will give you signals. If she's the quiet type, it's a good idea to ask her how she's feeling. Ask if it feels good. Make it sexy by whispering it in her ear. Talking dirty is always welcome. I dare you to find a woman who doesn't respond to hot little questions and suggestions. Even if they make her blush, she's still digging it. "Do you like it when I bite you like this? Does my finger against your asshole feel good? Do you want me to push it in?" Questions like these will do double duty by opening up a sexual dialogue as they turn her on.

The Best I've Ever Had...

As far as I'm concerned, anyone who truly loves pussy is going to eventually be great at licking it. All the truly awesome head I've gotten in my life has come from lovers who just couldn't get enough box. They loved, loved, loved it and would have had their faces in it 24/7 if they could have. They

Are your feet prepared for worship? Nothing's hotter than having an orally inclined lover nibbling at your toes. Make those tootsies mouth-worthy with these tips.

1. Soak them for a good 20 minutes in hot, soapy water. Relaxing in a bubble bath will get you all warm and ready for sex while preparing your feet for a pedicure.

2. Rub those calluses with a pumice stone. Or if you have major calluses, first scrape them lightly with a disposable razor, then sand them smooth. This is the most essential step. You want your feet to feel as smooth and sexy as the rest of you, so really go to town with that pumice.

3. Wash them carefully with something sweet and fresh-smelling, like peppermint- or lavender-scented body scrub. Try the Body Shop for great scented foot care products or check out your local drugstore.

4. Bag Balm is a petroleum-based goop (with lanolin) that you can buy at most drugstores. It's designed to prevent cow's udders from drying out and chapping. It works wonders on scratchy heels. Before bed, coat your footsies in a thick layer and cover them in heavy socks. In the morning you'll be soft enough to lick.

5. Paint your toes a bright, slutty red.

wouldn't even mind getting all pruny. Probably the best head I've ever had was from a woman who loved my hoo-hoo with such vehemence that she refused to stop once I'd climaxed. She just kept at it, licking and licking until I came again and again. No matter what I did, how I squirmed, how I tried to pry my snatch from her tongue, she just kept going. She kept me from getting overstimulated by constantly varying her technique. She'd pay attention to my clit for a while, then fuck my vaginal opening with her tongue, then nibble my inner lips, then lick lightly at my outer, and so on. She used her fingers in my cunt and in my ass. She stroked my thighs and belly. She touched me in every way you can possibly imagine. I must have had eight orgasms in the span of two hours. She claimed eating me out was her very favorite thing to do. One afternoon, as the sun beamed through my curtains onto our sex bed and we lay there exhausted after a marathon session of oral attention, my lover dozed next to me, happy and sticky. I was so thoroughly sated, I got up my nerve and gushingly exclaimed to that her she gave the best head I'd ever had in my life. She was so pleased, you would have thought that I'd handed the woman a check. She said it was the best compliment she'd ever received. And that being great at going down was her ultimate goal. No wonder she was so good at it!

How to Tell if You're Doing It Right

If she's groaning and leaning into your touch or pulling your hair or saying Yes! Yes! Yes! or otherwise showing enthusiasm, you're clearly doing something right. Begin to experiment with stronger stimulation. Bite her, pinch her, nibble her neck and earlobes, and give her ass a resounding slap (not too hard—you don't want to piss her off).

Once she's dripping wet and pleading with you, you can very slowly and gently begin licking the slit between her outer labia to make her cunt open up. Run your tongue up and down the length of her inner labia. Make sure to vary the pressure and pay close attention to her responses. She'll give you hints as to what feels best.

"My lover is always in skirts, and she often 'forgets' to wear underwear, so I have access to her pussy all the time. Last week we were dancing at a club and she got turned on and made me follow her into the bathroom and go down on her. She makes a lot of noise so I know the other women in the bathroom heard. But it was so hot I didn't care." —Carla

This little game of torture can be continued for as long as you like or until she starts pulling your hair and cursing at you. Fuck her with your tongue. It's wet, it's pink, it's muscular—it's made for fucking! Get that baby in there as far as it will go. Being probed by a wet tongue feels lovely, and using your tongue in that way is incredibly hot. Try it.

Don't pull her hood back to expose the glans just yet. Just give her some soft sweet strokes over and around it. Tease her and draw out the sensation. Make it last. Draw it out and don't give in. Tease her until she's ready to hate you.

Saliva is your friend. Use your mouth and tongue to keep the area as wet as possible. Moisten your fingers before touching her. It's not polite to put dry fingers in a pussy—just ask Emily Post. You can experiment with pulling back her hood with wet fingers. Expose her pink pearl and lightly lick it. Bury your face in her snatch and savor it. Really get in there. Act like you're trying to return to the womb.

She's going to feel so sexy and yummy with you eating her like that. Experiment with suction. Suck her button like a cock. Watch her face as you do this and try and gauge if she's responding to it. Not everyone will dig it, but many women will, and it's a great trick to bring more blood into the clit—making it extra hard and sensitive.

Are you paying attention? Does she like what you're doing? Ask her. If she's subtly trying to scooch away from you, you're probably applying too much pressure. Lighten up. Some women's clits are so sensitive that they don't enjoy direct stimulation at all. It feels ticklish to them or painful. If she's of this ilk, keep your licks light and next to or above the clit rather than directly on it. Big looping circles over and around her vulva feel great. But for those who can take it, small circles around the glans and up over the hood will quickly get them hot and bothered and eager for more.

Different Strokes, Different Folks

Here are some combos to try:

- Slow circles around the clit
- Looping figure eights around the entire vulva
- Small, hard circles around her knob
- Up and down, up and down, right on her button
- Small circles alternated with sideways licks
- Licking up and down, dragging your bottom lip over her clit with each upstroke
- Flicking your tongue back and forth over her clit like a porn star
- Sucking her clit into your mouth and flicking your tongue across it

- Pointed jabs at the top of her clit with a stiff tongue
- Rubbing your puckered lips over and around her knob
- Tongue-fucking her while using your nose to nuzzle her clit
- Wide, flat licks that use the entire tongue

Rhythm Nation

Finding a rhythm and staying with it is the key to making a woman come. Once you've gotten her to third base, the way to bring her home is to settle into an orgasmic groove. Groove to that Barry White CD you've got playing on the stereo and get a vibe going with your mouth. Find something she clearly responds to and stick with it, damn it.

Overstimulation

Too much of a good thing can be bad. She's got so many nerve endings down there that if you try too many fancy tricks, it's possible to overload her system. She may indicate this by pulling away or by shifting around. Ask her what's going on. Don't feel discouraged. You didn't do anything wrong. You've just sent her so many pleasurable sensations that her nerves went all crazy.

System overload can take the form of extreme sensitivity to the point of pain. Or it can be numbness. Either way, back off for a bit. Move your attention to another area—her nipples, her ass, her feet. Let her clit rest for a minute or two and get back to its normal sensitivity. She'll soon come back around and be ready to continue on to orgasm.

Don't Sprain Your Tongue!

There are many tricks you can employ if your tongue gets tired. Hopefully you've been pacing yourself and varying all your strokes up to this point. You've already brought your lips into play. If your tongue is at a stopping point and she's nowhere near home, use your lips to mimic the same rhythm your tongue was tapping. Or move your entire head around rather than just your tongue. Use your jaw and neck muscles to keep the movement going while giving your tongue a rest. If you get tired of that, rock your whole body up and down. Alternate this technique with tongue licks and you can keep going and going like the Energizer bunny.

A Straight Man Speaks

My good friend Ian is widely considered to be a pussy-licking master among straight and bi girls alike. Every girl I spoke to agreed, and a few even swooned. So I asked for his top 10 tips for becoming a rug-munching master:

1. Really enjoy it.
2. Don't look at it as obligation because she did you.
3. Love the power you wield as the source of her pleasure.
4. Pay close attention to what you're doing. Focus. Don't zone out.
5. Be aware of how she's responding. Understand that her pleasure centers can shift around from one time to the next.
6. Have stamina. Commit to being down there for as long as it takes.
7. Tease her for a long time before going anywhere near her clit.
8. Vary your strokes. Don't let her get bored.
9. Gradually build the intensity of your tongue work.
10. Bury your face in her snatch. Really show her how much you're enjoying it.

How to Read Her Body Language

Every woman is going to respond a little bit differently to sexual stimulation. But if you are paying attention, you can probably figure out what she wants from you based on the physical cues she's giving. Now, I can't claim to be an expert on every woman's reaction, but there are a few maneuvers that are pretty common. And remember, you can always ask!

- **She's grinding her hips:** She may be trying to get you to lick a little harder and or faster.
- **She's bucking her hips up and down against your face:** She wants more contact or faster, firmer tongue action.
- **She's pulling back from your mouth:** She needs a lighter touch. You are using too much pressure.
- **She's scooting her kitty right or left:** You probably aren't hitting her most sensitive spot. Adjust your tongue according to her movements until she seems satisfied.
- **She's curling her hips up toward your face:** Your tongue action is too high. Lick her a little lower.
- **She's pushing her hips down into the bed:** Your tongue's too low. Lick higher up, toward the top of her mons.
- **She twitches or jumps when you get too close to her clit:** Her clit is very sensitive. Avoid direct contact.

And Then She Goes Boom!

You should always be paying attention to her cues. Is she tensing up? Is her clit very erect? Is she flushing? When she's obviously climbing that hill toward orgasm, her thighs are crushing your head, she's grabbing at the sheets, she's screaming your name, whatever it is that she's doing...don't you dare stop what you're doing until she goes boom!

Once she's come, keep your lips in contact with her clit till her orgasm has completely subsided. If she's multiorgasmic, you'll want to give her the opportunity to show it. But don't keep licking until you know she wants to come again.

"I once had a boyfriend who was really good at it. Sometimes oral sex isn't enough to get me off. I'm a girl that likes to get fucked. But my ex, he could make me come really hard every time. I loved it more than I've ever loved it with anyone else. He once made me climax four times in a row. I guess that would have to be the best experience with cunnilingus I've ever had. Actually, now that I think about it, I really miss him!"
—Melissa

Don't Get Hurt!

Does she come like a bucking bronco? Do you have trouble staying on for more than eight seconds? Or does she squeeze your head between her thighs?

I had a lover who grabbed my head very tightly as she was about to climax. Her index fingers pressed against my temples, which was fine and in fact rather exciting. But from time to time, especially if she was nearing a really big orgasm, her pinky fingers would dig into the sides of my neck, cutting off the blood supply to my brain. I didn't want to stop the action and ruin her fun, so I'd be down there licking away like a good little lesbian, praying to some unknown deity that my lover would climax before I passed out. Several times she made me see stars. It was unintentional; she was just having a really good time, totally unaware that I was about to enter the light like Carol Ann. Of course I talked to her about it after she had come and had some time to settle down. She was extremely apologetic and promised to be more careful. But the next time I went south, the same thing happened. After a few near-death experiences I learned to adjust the angle of my head when I felt her getting close so my carotid arteries were safely out of reach.

If your girl thrashes around and gets your head in a death grip, try to carefully extricate yourself while keeping the action going. Try holding her hands down at her sides as you feel her getting close. If it's her crushing thighs you live in fear of, try pushing her legs apart with your hands as you lick her. And after she's come, find a nice way to bring it up that won't hurt her feelings. And be thankful that your honey's orgasms are such a good show.

What About That ABC Trick?

Does that old spell-out-the-alphabet-with-your-tongue trick actually work? Well, since it's repetitive but with a lot of variation, it could in theory make for a nice rhythm. But if you're concentrating that hard on the alphabet, how are you paying attention to her body clues? Unless you're a prodigy, stick with something simpler.

Is She a Hard Nut to Crack?

Let's assume that she's usually able to orgasm with a partner and not on muscle relaxants or Zoloft. Everything is going well, and she's into it and totally close, but she just can't get over that hump. Well, first, the most obvious thing is that she doesn't have to come. It's possible that she doesn't even want to, and pressuring her is only annoying her. Let her know that stopping is OK, if that's what she prefers. But what if she wants to, yet just can't quite do it?

Tricks to Help Make the Earth Finally Move

- Change your stroke (i.e., from circles to up-and-down licks, etc.).

- Use your hands to stimulate other erogenous zones: nipples, ass, feet...
- Stroke her belly to help her relax.
- Put your fingers in her cunt—as many as will fit. Make her feel filled.
- Stick a well-lubed finger in her ass and slowly fuck her with it.
- Move away from her clit for a few minutes. She could be overstimulated. Give her a brief break and then return to what you were doing.
- Hand her a small vibrator (like a pocket rocket or a mini vibe) to add to your tongue work.
- Moan or hum into her crotch.
- Push into her belly just above the pubic bone—applying external pressure to her uterus.
- Use your tongue and your fingers on her clit at the same time.

Tips for Tops

On my back with legs spread is the position I was born to be in—but obviously not all of us feel that way. So what do you do with someone who is usually on top but is eager to experience the wonders of your tongue? If you're the top and you think the idea of being licked into oblivion sounds great but you feel all weird giving it up like that, try ordering your little oral hottie around. If you're butch, tell her to suck your cock (if that's what you like to call it). Be demanding. Be dirty. Push her down and straddle her face. Or push her head between your legs and hold it there. There are many delightful ways to enjoy getting eaten out while still engaging in the dynamic you and your partner enjoy. The big love of my life put the *t* in top, and

Is Your Lover Transgendered?

Genitals and gender don't always coalesce the way we want them to. Your female lover could be male-bodied and have a bio-dick. Or your male lover might have a cunt. Gender is a spectrum and people can fall anywhere on it. If your lover is transgendered, communicate openly with him or her about how they would like their genitals treated and touched. I'm guessing whatever he or she calls it, they want your mouth on it!

she spent plenty of time on her back with my face between her thighs without once giving up her control or status as King Daddy. I loved every minute of it. She had me so trained that even thinking about going down on her would get me wet. So remember, getting done does not a bottom make. Tops get off too!

For Would-be Lickers

Is your lover of the receptively reluctant variety? Let's assume you want to make her feel good because she wants you to and not because you have something to prove. This isn't about power plays or flipping someone. It's about giving something to your lover that she truly would like to experience but doesn't feel comfortable asking for or can't quite relax into. If this is the case, there are many tricks and techniques you can try that will make the experience fun for both of you.

How does your lover relate to her cunt? Is she female-bodied but feels masculine? Ease her into oral heaven by sucking her cock. If she usually wears a strap-on, go down on that thing with as much delight and horny eagerness as you're feeling. Make your enjoyment obvious to her. Get her hot by looking up at her and letting her enjoy the visual of your mouth stretched around her tool. Use your fingers to sneak behind her strap-on and surreptitiously pleasure her pussy. Gauge her level of arousal. Some women can come this way. If she's able to do so, great! But if she needs direct stimulation of her clitoris, use her cock as a pleasure path until she's extremely turned on. When she's reached a point of no return, ask her to take it off. Or push it out of the way if that's possible. Once you've made contact, don't suddenly change your tactic and get all rough and ready. Remain girly—even submissive—if that's what she wants. Let her know how much desire you're feeling. Continue to work on her clit as if it were a cock. This is not a time to try out any fancy new moves. Shoving a couple of fingers in her cunt is only going to annoy her, or worse, piss her off. Just keep working her clit with your mouth. Look up at her, let her enjoy the visual of you working hard between her legs. Moan and groan and let yourself go. Don't pressure her to come. But if she's ready for this kind of experience, and you don't pull any crazy role switching on her, you just may make it happen.

Suck Dyke Cock

Giving your girl a strap-on blow job can be a searing-hot, pre-pussy-licking pleasure. Try sucking her dick, then easing her out of her harness and onto her back. Since dyke dick is largely psychological, you can help her get off on the visual thrill by putting on a show. These cocksucking tips are sure to get the party started:

1. Nibble and lick her thighs and belly, grab her ass, touch her all over before putting her cock in your mouth.
2. Tease her cock. Use all the same tricks you'd use before approaching her clit.

3. Treat her dildo as if it were a real dick. Lick it, tease it, circle the head of it with your tongue. Lick the underside. If it has balls, don't leave them out.
4. Keep everything visible. She's getting off on the view. Don't let your hair cover your face.
5. Look up at her while you suck her dick. Let her enjoy the way you look with her cock in your mouth
6. Wrap your hand around the base of her dildo and push it into her crotch as you suck.
7. Slide your mouth down on it as far as you can. Try and take all of it.
8. Slip some fingers behind her harness and tease her cunt while you suck.
9. Finger her butt hole.
10. Alternate your strokes. Don't get repetitive.

Five
Positions!

There are any number of positions two people can get into to enjoy a little knob jobbing. You just need an imagination and a willing partner. Hell, you don't even need a horizontal surface; just kneel in front of her, stick out your tongue, and nuzzle away—you can do that anywhere. But there are a few tried-and-true formations that have stood the test of time, and since they probably weren't covered in your high school sex ed class or on the Discovery Channel, I'm going to lay out a couple of them here.

Some of these positions may seem obvious; some will be new. But if you've been in a monogamous relationship for several years, and all you do is plop down on your back and spread your legs, then you probably need a few reminders about all the exciting formations you and your lucky licker could be creating. Sometimes monogamy, as wonderful as it is, leads to laziness and rote behavior in the bedroom. So, sweeties, you partnered pussy lickers need a little refresher course. And you single gals and guys need one as well. Don't be a one-trick pony, even when it's with a different pony every night.

Read this chapter and go do a few yoga stretches. Your pussy, or your lady's pussy, will thank you.

On Her Back

This classic position for dining at the Y has many wonderful benefits. As the licker, you have easy access to everything you need to have access to. You can reach up to touch her breasts, stroke her belly, and grab on to her hips to pull her muff closer to your face while you lick her. You can easily incorporate penetration in this position, so go ahead and stuff a few digits into her box or her ass. And, maybe most important, this position allows you the most access to her entire vulva. You aren't tethered by her body on top of you, and you control how close you can get to her. These are great things. She's reclining, which makes it easier for her to relax and go to her happy place. She can prop herself up on her elbows if she wants to increase the intimacy by making eye contact with you, and she can lie back down when that eye contact gets too intense. She isn't supporting her weight and doesn't have anything else to concentrate on besides the warm wet tongue gliding across her special purpose.

The one drawback of this one is that it can be a bit of a neck breaker. And if she's a slow comer, you risk serious neck strain. My friend Ian showed up to dinner at my place one night with the most curious posture. After some prodding about what caused his neck to bend in such a swanlike manner, he confessed that the night before, he crawled between the thighs of his lovely girlfriend and eagerly licked her magic nubbin for a full 90 minutes before she confessed she had taken a Flexeril for her pulled hamstring and probably wasn't going to reach fruition until her medication had worn off in four hours. So before you start, you should always ask yourself, *Am I going to be comfortable in this position for the next four hours?*

How It Looks

She lies on her back on the bed or some other comfortable horizontal surface. You lie on your stomach with your face between her legs and lick away. You can support your upper body weight with your arms by crossing them under your chest or propping yourself on your elbows. Or, if you prefer, cross your arms over her thighs or wrap them around her legs.

Variations

There are all sorts of various ways to add a little spice to this position. Push her knees up, or push just one knee up to change the angle of her vulva in relation to your tongue. Place pillows under her ass to raise her up. Have her put her feet on your shoulders. Or have her grab her own legs behind the knees and hold them up. Try the "Sex Sling," a piece of nylon webbing that goes behind her neck and under her knees, supporting the weight of her legs and allowing her to keep them in the air for extended periods of time. It's made by Sportsheets. It's a great little device to incorporate into extended periods of oral play, or anything else for that matter.

> *"My ex-lover and I mastered the art of 69 and the simultaneous orgasm. It's really a skill to match your bodies pussy-to-mouth on both ends and still be able to concentrate on giving good head. Plus she was a quick come, so in the beginning she'd get into getting off and lose focus on licking me. I was a good sport about it, of course. But I really wanted to make us come together. So after putting in many hours maneuvering our way across each other's body, we figured out that her on top, me underneath worked the best for getting and giving at the same time. The first time we had simultaneous O's I thought I'd died and gone to heaven. We loved doing it so much we even lost interest in fucking for a while."* —Mary

The Art of 69

Oh, yes, the ever-popular 69 position has many, many advantages, not the least of which is the simultaneous stimulation of both partners' genitals. Referring of course to the reciprocal positions of the participants' bodies, as in the number 69, this position requires one party to lie on his or her back while the other party lies on top in the opposite direction, thereby introducing a mouth to both pleasure zones. Reciprocal rug-munching side-by-side style instead of with one person on top is also called 69, just in case you were wondering.

This position is great because it's a two-player game, it

allows both parties access to the entire vulva, and the person lying on her back can easily reach her partner's cute little butt hole as well. It's often a little harder to get to the butt hole of the person lying down, but with some maneuvering you'll manage it.

Both partners in this position can control their reach, pulling their partner's naughty bits as close to their face as they like. This is also a great position if you want to penetrate your partner while you go downtown. If she's on top, her ass and cunt are in the air just waiting for a finger or two, or maybe a handheld dick or butt plug. If she's on her back, you can easily reach her cunt with fingers or a handheld cock.

This position is perfect for het couples because the woman can crawl on top and control the amount of cock she takes in her mouth, either choosing to showboat her deep-throat skills a bit or back off her gag reflex and take it easy. If she's on the bottom, she can easily reach her partner's asshole while she sucks him off. If he's eager for a little back-door action, well, great. But if he's nervous, then the 69 position might be just the way to introduce his ass to the thrill of your finger. When there's so much going on with your cunt in his face and his cock in your mouth, he won't have time to stop the action until he's already enjoying it. That little tip holds true for lesbians too. If either partner is a reluctant butt pirate, I say ease them into it with some hot, raucous sex and a few orgasms, and then trick them if you have to.

Sixty-nine does have a few minor drawbacks. Sometimes it's hard to concentrate on giving good head when you're getting close to the big O and vice versa. Sometimes extreme differences in height can make it difficult to reach your partner's cunt when yours is attached to her face. Also, for the top, it can be awkward to support your body weight for as long as two orgasms take.

How It Looks

One person lies on her back while the other person crawls on top facing the opposite way, uniting her mouth with the bottom's genitals and her genitals with the bottom's mouth. Voilà!

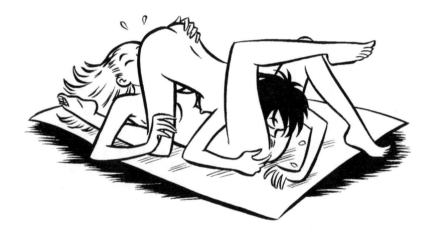

Variations

If your height difference prevents you from joining mouth to cunt on both ends, join mouth to cunt—or cock—on one end and fingers to cunt on the other. Perhaps your partner wants you to fuck her while she licks you? Maybe she wants to feel your fingers circling her clit. Try out a few different tricks until you figure out what she's craving. If you don't quickly realize what she wants...ask, silly! Don't be afraid to give her pleasure without focusing on orgasms.

Sixty-nine can be great foreplay fun. When one or both of you wants to come, it's OK to switch to another position that allows more focused access.

Seated

When your lady is sitting in a chair and you're kneeling between her legs, she gets to feel like a princess being serviced. Your head is within easy reach so she can indicate when she wants you to use more pressure by pulling your face closer to her cunt. She can direct your movements with her hands and pull your hair when she's really excited. Not only that, but she gets the added thrill of watching your tongue as it glides all over her snatch and hard clit. She can look down between her legs and see your tongue hard at work and watch her own body as it changes and responds to the stimulation. Sitting down allows her to relax and enjoy the show without worrying about supporting her weight or concentrating on your pleasure as well. In fact, all she has to do is relax, enjoy herself, and come.

For the licker, having your woman sitting down in front of you also allows you to see more of what's going on. Because you aren't prone, you have more freedom of movement. You can pull back and study her cunt up close and personal. It may just be the best view you can get of her special place. Go ahead and revel in the beauty of her hoo-hoo. Just don't stare in a clinical way and make her feel like she's at the gyno!

In this position you have a lot of access to her body; you can raise yourself up onto your knees to reach her breasts and kiss her mouth. You can wrap your hands around her thighs and caress her legs and hips. And if she leans back, you can easily fuck her vagina and ass with fingers or toys.

As long as you kneel on a pillow or something soft, there really are no drawbacks to this position. It's possible that the kneeling partner may feel as if the power dynamic is unbalanced, that is, perhaps they feel like an oral sex service bottom (um, hot!). So discuss any stuff like that when it comes up for you. Power dynamics can be especially exciting and add spice to any sexual activity. So if kneeling in front of her makes you feel submissive, try going with that feeling and see where it takes you.

How It Looks

Sit your girlfriend in a chair or at the end of the bed and kneel between her open thighs. Enjoy the sight of her wet snatch as you lick her to orgasmic bliss.

Variations

Try kneeling in front of your lady as she's standing up with her legs spread. This way you can grab her ass and really pull her cookie into your mouth. If she's a bigger girl, this position may not give you enough access to the vulva. Don't be afraid to spread her open with your fingers. Pull back on her mons to expose the little man in the boat. If it's not working out for either of you, worship her belly and thighs with your tongue, then have her lie back for the main event. Or try something else. Try sitting on the kitchen counter, at the edge of the tub, or on a comfy park bench.

Sit on My Face!

My friend Mike says, "Oh, he's a face hat" when he thinks a guy is hot. You can make your favorite chickie into a face hat by having her kneel over your head and crouch down against your face. This is a hot position. Next to 69, it's got the most skin-to-skin contact of any of the classics. She has all of the control. She can smother you with her wet box if you two are pervy that way, or she can pull back and dole out her clit to your tongue in tiny amounts, like a rich treat. You can reach up and grab her ass or wrap your hands around her thighs to pull her closer. There are all sorts of special sensory thrills with this position. Having your face pinned to the bed by her salty pink is extra yummy. And if her thighs are pressed to your ears and blocking out background sounds, all the better. Your pretty lady can gaze down at your face as you're hard at work. The view is hot, so give her a good show. Because your head is supported in this position, any fears she may have about you getting physically tired are allayed and she can more easily concentrate on the good feelings. She can choose how much mouth-to-cookie contact you have and can even take total control by fucking your face with her cunt rather than just simply accepting your oral ministrations. She can lean forward and support herself against the wall, headboard, edge of the couch, etc., depending on where you two are. Or she can sit straight up and gaze down at you. Encourage her to crouch over your face on all fours if it seems like her legs are tiring.

How It Looks

You lie on your back; she kneels on either side of your face, crouching low enough that her muff makes contact with your mouth.

Variations

She can kneel over you facing in the opposite direction so that her butt is right in your face if you like that kind of thing. She can even get onto all fours and crouch over you in a modified 69.

Sidelying

She can lie on her side and you can rest your head between her thighs, kind of making your head into the jam in a thigh sandwich. If you're worried she's going to squeeze her legs together, possibly snapping your neck when she comes, then her other leg can rest on your shoulders or torso. This is a really comfortable position and allows a good deal of access to her entire crotch. Plus it's all snuggly warm between her legs. She's relaxed, you're relaxed, everyone's having a great time, and no one is supporting his or her body weight or being smothered. You can easily use her legs as handles to pull her as close as you like. You can snuggle right up against her naughty parts or pull back to tease her a bit. Also, you can reach behind her and grab her ass. She can wrap her legs around you for added skin-on-skin contact. This is especially nice if your neck tends to get tired when she's on her back and you're between her legs. It has a similar feel to it, but it's less arduous.

How It Looks

She lies on her side and scissors her legs open. You rest your head on her thigh with your mouth pushed up against her clam. She then finds a suitable position for her other leg, either scissoring your head or hanging it over your shoulder. Fiddle around until it's comfortable.

Variations

You can come at her box from either side. This means that if you lie with your left ear against her thigh you'll be nose to clit. If you lie with your right ear against her thigh you'll be nose to perineum (or "taint," as some call it). This is a good position to offer both of you a bit of mobility. Try rolling around with each other while trying to stay connected. It's fun!

Doggy-Style

Doggy-style is a perennial fave. Really nothing beats it for pure aesthetic appeal. It's hot and naughty—plus the view is great! With her face in the pillow and her ass in the air, you can gaze lovingly at all the good stuff. She gets to feel like a dirty porn queen on all fours with her back arched, offering her body up for your oral worship. And you get to lick her stem to stern with no furniture or pillows or other body parts in the way. She's comfortable, you're comfortable, and most important, you have easy access to her ass! She can turn around and look at you or give you instructions. Or she can look straight ahead and concentrate on all the good feelings. You can get your face as close to her as you like or you can pull away and switch to fingers for a little variety. Depending on how bendy she is, you may have trouble getting to her clit. She should arch her

back as much as comfortable, and if you still need more access, lie on your back and dive under her in a modified sit-on-my-face formation. This is also a perfect position for rimming. I highly recommend it.

How It Looks

She gets on all fours and you approach her from behind.

Variations

Bend her over the couch. Or for added raunch appeal, she can bend over and grab onto a chair. Basically any position the two of you can get into that involves her being bent over and your face in her crotch is going to be a good one.

66 Great Places to Eat Pussy

Pool tables
Bar bathrooms
Under her desk at her office
The backseat
The front seat
At the movies
At the library
At her parents' house
At the mall
On the sofa
At the dining table
On the kitchen counter
Gallery openings
In the locker room
Shoe stores
Under the table at a restaurant
Deserted subway cars
Drive-through car washes
Airplanes
Trains
Buses
In a swimming pool
Picnic tables
The woods
In the shower/bathtub
Deserted playgrounds
The ocean
At a drive-in
Doughnut shops
In an elevator
Motel rooms
In a lake
In a garage

In your backyard
In a van
Porno theaters
In a hammock
Construction sites
Convents
Barns
On a motorcycle
At the *Vagina Monologues*
Sex clubs
Steam rooms and saunas
In a recliner
On a waterbed
Amusement park rides
Horse-drawn carriages
Dressing rooms
On a sailboat
At the opera
Caves
Deserted golf courses
In a hot tub
On the floor
In a classroom after hours
In a tent
On a baseball diamond
In the mountains
In an RV
Dungeons
On a rooftop
At a rest stop
On top of the Eiffel Tower
Helicopters
And, of course, in a bed!

Six
Penetration and Sex Toys

Cunnilingus with penetration is just like an '80s power ballad. Your tongue is dancing around doing a fancy bunch of Eddie Van Halen guitar licks, and your fingers are inside her creating a good, strong Michael Anthony bass line. The resulting hit will earn you a rock-god reputation.

Keep in mind that some women may enjoy being eaten out as a welcome break from fucking, so don't just assume she wants something inside her. Find out if she likes it first. How? Ask her, silly. *Read her body signals.* And even if she says "Yes, please!" to a little finger bang, you should still start out slowly. Don't be trying to shove your hand in there right away. You don't get extra points for speed.

Fingers are, of course, the perfect tool for prodding your sweetie. They're communicative; you can feel every little sensation, every ripple of her pussy. Also, they're flexible and can reach around to explore her secret spots. Please make sure they're well-groomed. Excessively long nails, nicks, cuts, and scratchy calluses can be hazardous for one or both parties. You should always make sure your hands are well-scrubbed (i.e., clean) and ready for action. You may have already deployed them to help pull back her clitoral hood or splay her inner labia. The next step is to make sure they're well-lubed. (She's probably dripping wet from the tongue bath you're giving her, but that doesn't mean you won't need it. Commercial lubricants have a cushioning effect that saliva can't duplicate.) Even the wettest of pussies can benefit from a little extra slipperiness. You can never have too much lube. It really improves everything. And for serious in-and-out, you'll need lube to keep from hurting her.

Keep latex gloves at the ready. A necessary component of safer sex, latex gloves also make your fingers smooth and slippery for decreased friction.

A lubed-up finger tickling her anus might be just the trick to send her over the edge. Try it and see! If you already have a favorite lube, that's great. But if you don't, you can refer to the lube chart on pages 91–92 for a quick lesson on which store-bought sex juices have the least annoying taste and smell. My personal preference is Liquid Silk. As far as I'm concerned, it works for everything from G spot stimulation to anal sex to fisting. But experiment until you find something you can both agree on.

Lube makes any sexual activity better. It's not a spice; it's a necessary component of sex. Vaginal lubrication cannot always be counted on, and most of the time women are wettest when they first get turned on, but halfway through the fucking it's been mostly wiped away. And you should never go anywhere near anyone's ass without lube.

Getting Started

Slip in a single digit and gauge her reaction. A groan of pleasure is a good sign. And if she's pressing herself down onto your hand, you can bet she wants more. Point that digit up toward the front of her love box and press against the vaginal wall while maintaining an in-and-out motion. Don't stop licking, of course!

Do the old "come hither" trick with curved fingers and wiggle them back and forth toward the front of her cooch. If she's into G spot play, then feel around for the bumpy, ridgy section toward the front of her vaginal wall. Curl your fingers up toward your tongue and work her G from the inside while your mouth works her clit from the out- *Lube is good.* side. Press firmly. If she feels like she needs to take a tinkle, assure her it's normal. After all, you *are* pressing on her urethra.

Add more fingers as you go, making sure to check in with her about what she wants. She may want you to keep thrusting. She may need you to concentrate on G spot pressure. She may want to feel filled up with more fingers. Go slowly, *pay attention to physical cues,* and communicate.

If it's the ass your finger's after, start slowly. Extra slowly. Hopefully you've warmed her up with a little tongue action at her back door. If not, try teasing it with lots of tiny circles before you go sticking anything in there. Use plenty of lube and a light touch. Lightly stroke her butt hole for a while. Pet it; let her anticipate the pleasure you're about to give her. The ass needs lots of coaxing. It's the shy, sensitive type. Give it gentleness and lots of honest communication, and you'll win its heart. Anal penetration isn't part of the oral sex power ballad. It's more like a James Taylor song. Or Joni Mitchell. The ass likes a little bit of poetry.

Once you've warmed her up sufficiently, you can try coaxing a finger past the gates of heaven. Tease her first with lots of light little circles around her pucker—or anything else you know drives her crazy—then begin to penetrate her by pressing your fingertip against her butt hole. If she's ready and willing, you'll feel her ass open up to accept it. Slide in just the tip and see how your partner likes it. If her reaction is favorable, push your finger farther up her bum. Keep your finger lubed up and slip it in and out slowly. As you feel her muscles relax, you can vary your movements and speed. Ask her how she likes it, and progress slowly. If she's really into it, you can add another finger. Aim for a slow in-and-out fucking motion, and whatever you do, keep licking!

"My boyfriend has a tried-and-true method that makes me come hard every time. He gives me lots of direct tongue-to-clit stimulation until I'm very close to coming. Normally, I can't come from clit licking alone. I tend to plateau as I get close. So when he senses I'm close but not over the hump, he backs off my clit and slowly begins teasing my ass with his finger. He lubes up with a little pussy juice and slips his finger superslowly into my ass. He then fucks me slowly with his finger while he goes back to licking my clit. I come like gang busters." —Monique

If your girl is game, filling both holes at the same time can be mind-blowing. One option for this activity is to have a finger in her ass and your thumb in her snatch. But experiment with different combinations of fingers and holes till you figure out the perfect finger-banging formation.

Toys for Twats

Fingers are wonderful and readily available. But sex toys can deliver a whole rainbow of fruit flavors. Toys are like condiments: They enhance the flavor of your entrée but certainly won't take the place of it. So don't be worried about using them. Even if the final stretch of her orgasm is powered by her Hitachi Magic Wand, she still needs you between her legs.

Keep your options open by investing in a few well-made sex toys. If you're on a budget, you'll just want the basics. A strong but small vibrator like the Pocket Rocket and a good firm silicone dildo, especially one with a G spot curve, are a great place to start. Stick with silicone because it's boilable and nonporous, which means you can sterilize it. Other mystery plastics and rubbers may cost less, but they break down much faster and bacteria can thrive on their porous surfaces. Glass is totally nonporous and superslippery—acrylic too!—so you can fuck for a long, long time without becoming sore.

Keep Your Toys Clean

Clean plastic vibrators with alcohol. Do not immerse battery vibes in water—they'll corrode! Silicone toys can be washed in soap and water or boiled, but the lazy woman's way to clean silicone toys is to stick them in the top rack of the dishwasher. Just make sure to empty it before your mom comes over. Rubber toys are porous and can harbor bacteria, so it's best to always cover them in condoms. Clean them with soap and water and let them air dry.

Intro to Lube

There are three basic varieties of lube: Silicone, water-based, and oil-based. Each type has its own pluses and minuses.

Your Well-Stocked Sex-Toy Chest Should Contain These Basic Items

- a roll of Saran Wrap (for safer licking and improvised bondage)
- dental dams and condoms
- a vibrator small enough to use during intercourse (the Pocket Rocket is a good choice)
- a silicone dildo with a flared base (so you can use it in either hole)
- a small silicone butt plug
- nipple clamps

Luxury Items

- Hitachi Magic Wand (because a wand is a terrible thing to waste)
- a curved G spot stimulator
- an insertable glass or acrylic toy
- a bullet vibe (Stick it in a condom and stuff it up whatever hole you choose. Just make sure to pull it out by the condom, and not by the cord!)
- restraints of some type (fur-lined are comfy!)
- a blindfold
- alarger butt plug (for overachievers)
- a dildo harness (essential for dyke couples, but more and more het lovers are discovering the joys of strapping it on)

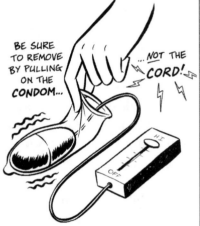

BE SURE TO REMOVE BY PULLING ON THE CONDOM... ...*NOT* THE *CORD!*

If you'd like to use the same toy anally and vaginally or be able to swap it with your honey, put a condom on it. Use a fresh condom for each hole the toy goes near.

Water-based lubes are suitable for all types of sex. They dry quickly but can be revived with a spritz of water or saliva. They often contain glycerin, which has been known to cause yeast infections, though these days more and more manufacturers are creating glycerin-free lubes. Read the ingredients. Water-based lubes are compatible with all safer-sex supplies and sex toys.

Silicone lubes feel great and stay slippery much, much longer. They are totally waterproof—great for hot tub parties. But they don't wash off very easily. I've found myself still slippery post-sleep and shower. They are compatible with everything except silicone sex toys. Never use silicone lube with silicone sex toys. The lube will erode the surface of the toy.

Oil-based lubes are best used for sensual massage, hand jobs for guys, and a little finger-up-the-bum action now and then—*but not for penetrative vaginal sex.* They just aren't very good for your kitty.

There are lots of lubes on the market. You'll have to experiment to find your favorite. But here's a rundown of some of the most popular ones:

Liquid Silk: Water-based. Creamy, soaks in to the skin like hand lotion. Lasts a long time. Never gets sticky. Has virtually no smell and a very mild taste.
Eros Water: No taste or smell. Doesn't get sticky. Lasts a long time.
Astroglide: Thin and sweet. Very slippery. Sticky. Contains glycerin.
Slippery Stuff: No taste or smell. Very slippery.
ID Juicy Lube: Comes in all sorts of weird fruit flavors. Very sweet. Contains glycerin. Can make your butt hole taste like strawberries.

Probe: Great all-around lube. Very thick and slippery. Slightly sweet chemical taste.

Maximus: Thick and cushiony. Great for anal sex. Mostly tasteless. Has no odor. All-around great lube. Very similar to Liquid Silk; made by the same company.

Eros: Light and superslick silicone lube. Stays on forever. Can also be used on noisy hinges.

Foreplay Lube de Luxe Cream: Thick and gooey. Slightly sweet.

O'My: Very sweet and sticky. Touted as an all-natural choice. Contains botanicals that claim to enhance arousal.

Wet: Very thin. Sweet chemical taste.

Sensual Power: Creamy, lotion-like lube. Long-lasting. Minimal taste. Loved by fans of Liquid Silk.

Hydra-smooth: Glycerin-free. Creamy. Minimal taste. Lotion-like. Not sticky.

Elbow Grease Hot Gel: Slippery, long-lasting. Contains menthol for added sensation.

Embrace Unflavored: Thick. Slightly sweet.

Pleasureglide: Slick, smooth. Slight chemical taste.

KY Jelly: Kind of grossly thick. Reminds me of going to the gyno. However, you can get it anywhere, including Texas.

KY Warming lube: Very thin. Not too sticky. Slight chemical taste. Too thin for serious hoo-hoo banging, but the warming effect adds a nice sensation to masturbation.

Sensua Organics: Totally organic, all natural ingredients. Comes in flavored and unflavored. Slippery, not too sticky. The flavored tastes sweet; the unflavored tastes a tiny bit bitter.

Pick up the Vibe

If your lady friend has trouble climaxing, adding a vibrator to your sex play can take the pressure off both of you.

She'll know an orgasm awaits her, and that will relieve her stress level, allowing her to concentrate better on the wonderful job your tongue is doing. And with the wand that goes buzz at the ready, you can both be confident that she'll come before your face falls off. Don't feel shy about including this tool. Many, many women prefer to come with one. It doesn't mean you are—or that she is—inadequate. It simply means she likes the buzz. You can alternate vibration with tongue action, or think of the vibrator as the closing relief pitcher. Lick her till the bottom of the ninth, then bring in the magic arm. Now, *that's* throwing her a curve!

Insertable vibrators can really add some extra-special sensation to an oral session. Try any type of insertable vibe whose shape you find appealing. Long, hard plastic slimlines are great. They're a classic, and they come in just about every color and pattern imaginable. I personally own one in silver, one in leop-ard print, and one in pink sparkles, because I never know what color lingerie I'll be wearing, and I like to match my toys to my outfit.

Angled G spot toys are another great option for extra fun. They feel great, and they may make your girl gush in a way she never knew she could. The first time a lover tongued me while she fucked me with a G spot-curved dildo, I came so hard she could have drowned. Consider yourself warned.

Anything curved and firm is a good option for pushing on her magic G, but certain toys are specially designed to hit "the spot." Many people swear by the Vixen Creations G spot attachment for the head of a Hitachi Magic Wand. Its only drawback is that it's cumbersome and can be difficult to use while you're licking her box. The Crystal Wand is another winner. It's 10 inches of curved Lucite specially designed to reach her magic spot. It's thin and easily maneuverable so you can keep it out of the way of your tongue. Also, its small circumference ensures that it won't get in the way of her ejaculation—should she be so inclined.

"Ihave a pink jelly rubber G spot vibrator that really makes me gush. I like it when my girlfriend fucks me with it while she licks my pussy. I really squirt a lot. It's not just a few tablespoons that come out—it's like a cup or more of liquid. She occasionally gets shot in the face. I used to feel bad about that until she convinced me that she loved it."
—Sophie

Butt Plugs

Butt plugs offer a cute, hands-free way to fill her up. Pop one in and lick away. She gets the throbby little zing of anal  stim, and you don't have to work any harder. Try pressing a vibrator to the base of a silicone butt plug. Silicone transmits vibrations very well, so this little trick can make her do backflips. Anal beads are another good-time toy. Stuff them up her bum and then pop them out one at a time as she nears orgasm, or pull them out all at once as she comes.

Vixen Creations makes a great set of anal beads that are hand-dipped in silicone. They clean up extremely easily and can be sterilized. If you buy plastic beads, check first for any hard ridges. Nothing sharp should ever go near the ass. It's delicate in there.

You can also fuck her ass with a dildo of whatever size and shape she desires. Use liberal amounts of lube on any toy that's going in her ass. Remember: Anything that goes in must have a flared base. Remember that old wives' tale about things getting sucked up into the ass and lost? Well, that's not urban folklore, baby! It happens.

Clamps

I love nipple clamps. Not only do they have a delightfully kinky feel, but the ones with a chain running between them are extremely versatile. Clamp her nips and tug on the chain with your hand while you nuzzle her box. Or try clamping them to her inner or outer labia, then tugging away while you're licking her clit. Don't leave clamps on for too long. The longer they are on, the more painful it will be when they come off. Twenty minutes or less is a good rule of thumb.

Female Ejaculation for Lovers

Female ejaculation is more than a neat party trick. It's also empowering and totally hot. It's visible proof she caught the brass ring. Want to make her squirt like a garden hose? Well, try this.

First, the would-be squirter should go take a tink. If she's new to G spot play, the sensations can be confused with the need to pee. If her bladder is empty, she'll have less to worry about.

If she's never squirted before, then choose an angled G spot toy for this exercise. Fingers or a fist also work, but toys are easier to maneuver.

Warm her up in the usual manner. Fondle, caress, and kiss her. Do what it takes to get her turned on. Talk dirty. Whisper sweet nothings in her ear about what a beautiful, nasty slut she is—or whatever she responds to. Go down on her. Lick her lovingly. Get her hot and bothered. Eat her out until she's close, but don't let her come just yet.

Stick two well-lubed fingers into her and feel around toward the roof of her vag. Aim for the ridged, bumpy area just about an inch or two inside and press firmly. The G spot gets firm and fills with fluid only when she's very aroused. The hotter she is, the more prominent her G will be, and the more likely she'll be to squirt. Drag your fingers back and forth over her spot as you continue your tongue action. Keep stimulating it. She may feel like she has to pee. She doesn't. It feels that way because the G spot, also known as the periurethral sponge, surrounds her urethra. So when you stimulate it, you're also stimulating her urethra. Talk to her; check in and see how's she's feeling. Does she want more pressure? Less? Just ask!

Once you've gotten a feel for where her G spot is and how much pressure feels good to her, take out your G spot toy of choice and lube it up.

As you lick her, fuck her firmly with the toy, keeping most of the pressure toward the front wall of her pussy. As she gets close to orgasm she will probably begin to bear down, effectively pushing the toy out of her box. You should continue to push back until the moment of orgasm. Let her push it out as she comes. Don't push it in; you'll block the flow. This is a timing trick. You want the toy out of the way of her flow, but not before she's riding the orgasmic wave. Pull it out at the right time and don't be surprised if you get a faceful of girl juice!

Keep in mind: All women are different, so there's no guarantee it'll happen. Not everyone enjoys G spot play. And pressuring your partner to squirt will only piss her off. Try these tips only if all parties agree they want a gusher.

"My wife had gotten hold of a copy of a video called How to Female Ejaculate, *and we thought we'd give it a try. Now, if I had known she was such a quick study I would have worn my snorkel, because with just the right combination of dildo and tongue action our bed became an underwater wonderland."* —Jack

For Would-be Gushers

Hopefully, all this attention to your G feels good. And if it doesn't, you should have said something by now. You've emptied your bladder, so ignore any signals your body may be giving you that you still have to pee. You don't. Whatever happens is going to be fun, so concentrate on letting go.

The big difference, in my experience, between squirters and nonsquirters is whether they push out or pull in during the big O. Squirting requires you to bear down and push out during orgasm rather than clench your muscles and pulling in. So push out as your partner fucks you, and enjoy the feeling of the G spot toy dragging against your special love button. When the time comes to come, bear down through your orgasm and let the magic flow.

If it doesn't work the first time...well, you had fun, didn't you? Just try, try again.

G! My Puss Feels Terrific!

Learn more about G spot play with these educational G spot videos:

G Marks the Spot
Director: Lena Haas [Sexpositive Productions, 2003]

How to Female Ejaculate: Find Your G-Spot
Director: Nan Kinney [Fatale Video, 1992]

Magic of Female Ejaculation
Director: Dorrie Lane [House O' Chicks, 2002]

The Guide to G-Spots and Multiples: The Ultimate O
Director: none [Sinclair Intimacy Institute, 1995]

Seven

Free Your Mind and Your Ass Will Follow

Anilingus, also known as rimming, is the fine art of eating ass. Why eat ass, you ask? Because, duh, it's fun. It's hot, a little naughty, and feels great. And it's not just for fags anymore. Ass-licking is on the verge of becoming the sexual practice of open-minded lovers everywhere. Trust me, becoming a great lay is all about the ass, baby. Want to go down in history as the mouth that blew her mind? Eat her ass. And hey, if you're licking pussy, you're down there anyway, so why not give the pink star a little attention?

If anal penetration is on the menu, rimming is a surefire way to warm her up. And if she's nervous about getting fucked in the ass, starting her out with a slippery, soft tongue might just get her excited enough to crave it.

I remember clearly the first time someone went near my ass with her tongue. I was lying on my stomach in bed with my lover. She was nibbling and biting my ass and generally hovering around down there with what were obviously prurient intentions. I was already feeling nervous and excited that so much attention was being paid to my ass. But I was totally unprepared for her wet mouth right up against my pucker! I nearly died from pleasure. It was all juicy, squishy loveliness going on around my supersensitive private place. I loved it, but of course, it was hard to remain relaxed. I worried about my smell and taste, and I kept trying to squirm away from her tongue. In my mind, there was no way she could be enjoying what she was doing.

Lucky for me, she sensed the insecurity behind my reluctance and refused to cease and desist. She held me down. I gave in and relaxed—then whoa! From that day on, my world was rocked. I was a huge fan of that act and that lady from that point on. Her eager tongue has earned her a place on my list of all-time greatest lovers.

We all know that the butt hole is an extra-sensitive, nerve-filled enigma and a pathway to extreme pleasure. But sadly, it often doesn't get the attention it deserves. It's like the wistful little wallflower at the homecoming dance. She's secretly an animal in bed, but no one will take her home and find out because they're too afraid of what their friends will think.

I've seen even enlightened sex-positive types blanch at the thought of sticking their tongue between someone's ass cheeks or having a tongue down around their own little wallflower. Boy, are they ever missing out! Rimming can add a whole new spectrum of pleasure to a session of oral sex. Your butt hole is an extremely responsive, horny little slut. Even the tiniest little touches can register high on the sensation scale. Learn to treat it right, and it can become a pathway to Nirvana.

It's true that there are a lot of taboos surrounding the ass as a place of sexual pleasure. Some people think that enjoying a little tushy attention means they're a big ol' pervert or a slut or a weirdo. Some people can't get past the idea that the butt is a dirty place. And other people may actually dream of uniting a slippery, wet tongue with a sensitive butt hole, but they're way too intimidated to talk about it. Well, let's face it. The world is a dirty place. There may be lots of taboos surrounding any type of anal stimulation, but breaking taboos is half the fun of great sex.

Be a great lay. Learn to love the ass.

Get Over Your Hang-ups and Embrace Your Butt

The first step in having fun with your ass is becoming friends with it. Get to know your butt; learn to love it and relax it. We carry a lot of tension down there. You'd be surprised at just how much. Most of us are walking around with a tightly clenched asshole. It's a repository for stress, just like the jaw, neck, and shoulders. When our upper body is tense, we realize it and try to relax. Learning to do the same thing with your butt hole is the first step toward getting into butt-licking fun. So relax, relax, relax.

Try this exercise: Take a deep breath and hold it. Tightly clench your butt hole closed. Really squeeze it hard. Hold for a count of 10 seconds. Exhale and release the tension in your ass at the same time. Do this a few times. Then do a series of quick little clenches—open, close, open, close—as fast as you can. Try to clench and release 10 consecutive times. Then consciously relax your sphincter as much as possible. How do you feel? Lighter? More open? Good.

Next stop, a hot bath. We're going on a little exploratory mission that should help you learn to love your butt hole.

While your bath is running, take a good long look at your anus in a hand mirror. Your partner is going to have his or her mouth down there, and getting familiar with what they will be looking at is a good way to feel more secure.

You've probably got some hair growing around your anus. Everyone does. It's totally normal. If you don't like it, shave it, wax it, or use some other method to make your pucker hair-free.

Get into your hot bath and relax a few minutes. Think about how squeaky clean you're going to be and how awesome your partner's tongue is going to feel pressed up against your asshole. Wash your pussy and ass with a mild nondeodorant soap. Remember what you learned in Chapter 3? Deodorant soaps are irritating to your sensitive tissues. So use something gentle.

Gently lather up your butt hole and run your finger all around it. Press lightly against your hole and feel yourself open up. Once you're used to the sensation, stick that soapy finger where the sun don't shine and wash the first inch or so inside your ass. Probe your butt hole with that soapy finger, fuck yourself a little. This is a great way to help your anus relax and prepare it for the pleasures to come. Rinse well. You'll be super-squeaky clean and prepared for anything. Just so you know, a freshly washed asshole is about as clean as your garden variety vagina, and we lick that all the time.

News for Clean Freaks

Anal exploring does not necessarily mean you'll come into contact with shit, and even if you do, so what? Get over your fear of encountering shit. It's not that big of a deal. Everything is washable, and prudes are not sexy. You can always rely on a latex barrier for a cootie-free experience. And if you're planning on rimming a casual partner, I highly suggest using a barrier anyway. There's nothing hot about unsafe sex.

If you feel really nervous about the cleanliness of your ass, you can give yourself an enema. An enema washes any minute traces of poop out of the anal canal. It's not necessary, but if it makes you feel better, go for it. And some people find enemas exciting in their own right.

There are several options for giving yourself a little spring cleaning down there. The simple and cute little bulb syringe is probably the easiest and least invasive type of enema. It looks like a turkey baster. You can buy one at most drugstores and well-stocked sex-toy stores. Or check online. Suck warm water up into the bulb and squirt it up your well-lubed ass while sitting on the toilet. Release the water and repeat the process a few times until you feel sufficiently clean. Give yourself an hour or so to recover before your partner goes south. There may be a bit of water still inside you and you'll want to allow enough time for it to be reabsorbed. Also, your ass has a protective mucosal lining, and an enema washes it away. You'll want to give your body time to rebuild this protective barrier.

Another type of enema is the enema bag or hot water bottle enema, also available at drugstores. This one is trickier. It consists of an enema bag that you hang over the shower rod. The enema bag is attached to a long tube with a nozzle on the end. Fill the bag with warm water and hang it. Find a comfortable position. The classic position involves lying on your left side with your right leg bent toward your chest. Kneeling in the tub with your ass in the air is also good. Insert the lubed-up tip into your butt hole and release the clamp on the tubing. You will feel yourself gradually filling with water. Once you feel full, remove the tube and release the water into the toilet. Repeat this process until the water runs clear.

A third type of enema—the shower nozzle attachment enema—is more involved than the other two and really most practical for people who want to have enemas on a regular basis. You can buy the showerhead attachment through many popular sex shops. It's made of stainless steel and consists of a nozzle attached to a long flexible tube. The process is the same as with an enema bag; insert the lubed-up nozzle and let the water flow until you feel full, then release it into the toilet. Just be very careful about the water temperature and pressure. For more information on enemas, check out Tristan Taormino's excellent book *The Ultimate Guide to Anal Sex for Women*.

Never use store-bought enemas unless you dump the solution they contain and refill them with plain warm water. Store-bought enemas have nasty chemicals in them that are not at all good for you. They will irritate the lining of your ass and taste terrible on your partner's tongue. The whole point of giving your ass a little spritz is to make it a nicer place to lick. So stay away from terrible-tasting chemicals.

So now you've washed and rinsed, and your ass is clean enough to eat salad off of. Great! Get ready to have your mind blown.

"I'm a dyke, but I feel like a faggot when I'm licking my girl-friend's ass. There's something about having my mouth on her butt hole that's extremely exciting. My favorite part is her reactions. I get so hot when she clutches the sheets and tries to squirm away from me. The first time I did it, I nearly came from the visual thrill of her in front of me with her ass in the air. I think the fact that it's considered 'dirty' makes it feel extra hot. I always tell her what a naughty girl she is and how only dirty sluts let people lick their assholes. She really goes for that. Also, rimming her is a good precursor to butt fucking. I like to get her all prepped with my tongue and then stick my cock in her and fuck her really hard." —Kelly

Positions for Ass Eating

Most of the positions we discussed in chapter 6 can easily be adapted to ass-licking. Doggy-style is particularly good and allows your partner a fabulous view of your anus and pussy simultaneously. If you're a furry sort and not interested in shaving, then doggy-style allows your partner to spread your butt cheeks apart and have more access to your cute little starfish with less hair to impede the path.

On your stomach with pillows under your hips is good too. Handcuffing her hands behind her back will keep her from squirming away. We will cover restraints thoroughly in the next chapter. I just thought I'd throw it out there to get your imagination going.

The lickee on her back with legs in the air is also great. Just push her cheeks apart and lick away. Try bending her over something like a couch or chair and kneeling behind her. She can lie on her side with one knee pulled up to her chest and you can come at her from the side.

Experiment with different positions until you figure out what works best for you.

How to Eat Ass

Oh, honey, you're about to encounter a smooth, slippery, quivering little opening to heaven. Her reactions are going to drive your actions, so pay close attention. When I'm approaching a woman's asshole, the first thing I'm thinking about, before any tongue-to-skin contact is made, is how much pleasure I'm going to give her. I know I'm about to drive her crazy, and I know she's probably nervous and anxious waiting for the first little warm lick. I like to stretch it out and make it last. Toying with her anxiousness is good. You're in control; work it.

When using a barrier, always put some lube on the underside so the lickee enjoys a "wet tongue" sensation.

Now, we know that the little lady in front of you has just had a nice hot shower or bath, and she's all squeaky clean for your licking pleasure. So there's no reason to worry about encountering feces. Let's assume any ambivalence you might feel about licking ass has been dealt with. And if you and your lickee are not partnered, then you're practicing safer sex and licking her ass through a latex (or Saran Wrap) barrier anyway.

Most people's ambivalence about licking butt has to do with fear of encountering germs and nastiness. Just to put your mind at ease, let me assure you that your tongue can't really reach very far into her ass. Maybe an inch or so, tops. And for you to encounter shit, you'd have to be able to reach much, much farther up. The anal canal is merely a way station. If she's freshly bathed, your chances of encountering anything nasty are pretty slim.

Don't go right for the bull's-eye. Spread the love around

a bit. Nibble her butt cheeks; spank her a little. Kiss and lick the backs of her thighs and tease the crack of her ass with your lips and tongue. Slowly and deliberately spread her cheeks and put a few warm little kisses against her pucker. Tease the entire furrow of her ass with your tongue, lightly running it up and down. Then gently tickle her anus with your tongue, licking around and up and down. Gauge what she likes by her reaction. If she's moaning and groaning and leaning into it, you're doing great.

Ass-Eating Techniques to Try at Home

- Lick her from top to bottom, like an ice cream cone.
- Pucker up, buttercup, and place a bunch of fluttery little kisses against her butt hole.
- Flick your tongue quickly back and forth across her pucker.
- Rim around and around in circles.
- Give her an up-and-down, side-to-side combo move.
- Press the flat of your tongue firmly against her hole.
- Lick her firmly, lightly penetrating.
- Fuck her with your tongue.
- Dart your tongue lightly in and out of her hole.

Rim Safely

To prevent the spread of bacteria, once you've licked her ass, stay away from her pussy. If you want to go back to licking her coochie, get up and use mouthwash. Her pussy is delicate and easily prone to infection, and bacteria from her ass can cause a whole slew of problems.

Also, rimming should always be a pre-penetration activity. Don't eat her ass after you've fucked her. A vigorous fucking can drag bacteria to the outside of even the most carefully washed butt hole.

Rimming is not considered a high-risk activity for the

spread of HIV. However, unprotected rimming carries the same risks as unprotected cunnilingus, with the added possibility of transmitting hepatitis A. So rim safely. Dental dams, Saran Wrap, cut-open condoms, and latex gloves all make great safer-sex barriers.

Eight
Health Concerns

When it comes to passing along sexually transmitted diseases, cunnilingus is less risky than unprotected anal or vaginal intercourse (with shared toys or with a bio-cock or fingers). But that's not to say rug-munching carries no risks. And the whole myth that sisters of the sapphic persuasion can't get STDs from each other is completely untrue—especially if she's menstruating, when the risk of transmitting any and all STDs increases.

The vagina is a warm, moist environment; it's a nearly perfect place for bacteria to grow. And guess what? So is the throat. Any infection she can get in her snapper, you can get orally. So keep that in mind when you're dining at every Y in town. Oral sex is a great thing. But it *is* sex. And it carries risks.

We all say we're using dams and gloves every time. But are we *really* doing it? *Every* time? People slip up. So know the risks, and approach every new coochie as educated and prepared as you can be. Knowledge is power, and being powerful is hot.

No one is completely safe. And STDs don't discriminate by sexual orientation. If you're sexually active, no matter what that means to you, you're probably at risk for contracting an STD of some kind. Studies have shown that cheating partners often don't use protection because they aren't used to it or they aren't prepared.

By definition, an STD is an infection that's spread primarily by sexual contact: oral, anal, or vaginal, either by skin-to-skin contact or by exchanging bodily fluids, such as blood, vaginal secretions, or semen. If you're going down on a woman, you're exchanging bodily fluids—her pussy juice and your spit and everything that lives in them.

HPV

HPV, the human papillomavirus, may be the most common STD. It's practically epidemic on college campuses. And a whopping 70% of the adult population is infected. This thing is everywhere, and you don't want to get it.

HPV can be passed from woman to woman by skin or mucous membrane contact—the pussy and mouth are both mucous membranes. You can touch your pussy, give your fingers to your girlfriend to suck, and potentially transfer the virus to her. HPV can cause genital warts and cervical neoplasia (precancerous or cancerous cells). If you don't know your partner's entire sexual history, I recommend protecting yourself. The tricky thing about this little bugger is that it is nearly impossible to track. Most people carrying this virus show no symptoms. People can carry it around and pass it on and never even know they have it. This virus is so fucked up that there are no tests you can take when you're asymptomatic that will tell you if you have it. In other words, you won't know until you break out in a bunch of little bumps.

There is no treatment for HPV, but if warts develop they

can be burned off with liquid nitrogen. Having your bare ass in the air as the doctor touches your sensitive bits with liquid nitrogen does not sound fun. This is why we use dental dams.

HPV can be passed by fingers, so if you like a little penetration with your oral loving, use gloves. Some experts think that it can be passed by inserting toys, so to be safe, use a condom and clean all of your toys with anti-bacterial soap. All women need regular Pap smears and checkups, in part because Pap smears can detect HPV and cervical irregularities. Frequent Pap smears are particularly important if you're sleeping with a woman who is infected with HPV.

Bacterial Vaginosis

Bacterial vaginosis is one of the most common STDs among lesbians. It is a bacterial infection of the vagina spread through sexual contact. Your partner can give it to you by, say, rimming you and then licking your pussy. Or by sneaking a finger into your ass while she's going down on you, and then forgetting which finger it was and sticking it in your cunt. You can also get it by wiping improperly, douching, and using harsh soap, which leave you vulnerable to infection. The thing about BV is that you may not know you have it, but you will probably know something is wrong. Your smell and taste will be different. In fact, they will probably be foul. If your normally eager rug muncher is hiding from your cooze or holding her nose, chances are very high that an infection is present. A round of antibiotics usually clears it up.

Chlamydia, Gonorrhea, Syphilis

Chlamydia, gonorrhea and syphilis are bacterial infections and can be treated with antibiotics. All three can be passed by oral, anal, or vaginal sex. If she has an infection and you have a sore in your mouth, you can catch it. Sharing a dildo or sex toy—a good reason to use condoms on your toys—can also pass bacterial infections. Untreated chlamydia can cause long-term problems, including pelvic inflammation, swollen or scarred fallopian tubes, and chronic pain. Gonorrhea can cause many problems, including sterility, and syphilis can cause death.

Hepatitis

Hepatitis means "inflammation of the liver." There are many different strains of viral hepatitis. The most common are hepatitis A, B, and C. Hep A and B are not usually chronic, but hep C becomes chronic in about 85% of those who are infected. Hep A is transmitted via fecal matter to the mouth, so ass licking is especially hazardous. More flexible, hep B lives in all body fluids, including semen, blood, saliva, and vaginal fluids. It can be transmitted by any sexual contact. Hep C, transmitted only by blood, can be passed by sharing needles (or any intravenous drug paraphernalia), straws (e.g., for snorting cocaine), razors, and even toothbrushes. You can contract hep C by performing oral sex on a woman who is menstruating. Cuts or hangnails can also provide a pathway for hep C.

Hep A and B usually cause recognizable symptoms (such as jaundice), but hep C can remain asymptomatic for years. People can live with it for decades and suddenly find out that they have cirrhosis or fibrosis (scarring of the liver).

Herpes

Herpes sucks. It has no cure, and it's really contagious. You can spread it easily with mouth-to-box contact. In fact, you can spread it with finger-to-box contact or finger-to-ass contact or finger-to-mouth-to-box contact. You get the picture. A herpes breakout can range from a whole group of really painful sores to just one teeny little sore that you can't even really see. The virus is contagious only during the shedding cycle, but this includes the period right before the sores break out, so it's difficult to be completely sure.

HIV

HIV is still the scariest STD out there. The Centers for Disease Control and Prevention reports that 98% of HIV-positive women who have sex only with women also reported other risky behaviors, usually injection drug use. Female-to-female transmission of HIV may be rare, but there is still some risk. And the figures are skewed anyway because the CDC considers only women who have not had sex with a man in the last 12 years to be lesbian (for the purpose of reporting statistics). Hell, that excludes half my dyke friend base right there. You may think you're a lesbian, but the CDC doesn't see it that way. So we're going around quoting statistics that don't even apply to us.

Listen up. The inside of your mouth is a mucous membrane. If you have sores or cuts that come in contact with vaginal secretions or blood containing HIV, you're putting yourself at risk.

Dental dams, condoms, and latex or polyurethane gloves can block the transmission of HIV during sex. But one of the top ways of preventing HIV transmission is to know your partner's status. Get tested.

Dams Are Fun

Many people think using barriers for oral sex will ruin the mood. They just assume that licking a piece of latex will suck, and either find themselves opting out altogether on oral sex or taking risks they shouldn't take. Well, dams don't suck. They can even be kind of fun. Dental dams were, of course, designed for use by dentists. And true dental dams aren't all that appealing. They are kind of thick and rubbery, too small to cover much area, and don't transmit that much sensation. However, some smart sex-toy makers came up with dental dams designed especially for sex. I highly recommend the Glyde Dams. They are sheer 10-by-16-inch sheets of ultrathin latex. They even come in lots of fun flavors. It's a good idea to put a dollop of lube on the pussy side of the dam to give her an extra bit of slippery sensation. Also, you may want to mark the side you are licking with a pen. This helps prevent mix-ups should things get messy.

Another trick is to use plastic wrap as a barrier. It's cheap! Hell, it's probably already in your kitchen drawer. It's far thinner than latex, and it's transparent, so you won't lose any of the wonderful visual stimulation you get from gazing at her hard clit. You can pull off as much as you need and cover her entire crotch—allowing you to lick her ass to pussy and back again with no fear of transmitting bacteria.

Holding a Dam in Place

The trickiest thing about dental dams is holding the little buggers in place while your hands are busy elsewhere. One tried-and-true trick for crafty babes is to turn a garter belt into a dam holder. Hook each corner of the dam to a garter. Make sure to shorten the garters so that the dam fits snugly against your mound. Also, specially made dental dam holders are available from sex-toy retailers.

Using a barrier can make rimming more appealing. If you're worried about cooties or shy about smell and taste, cover her up in Saran Wrap and lick her worry-free. And arriers make pussy-licking safe even when she's having her period.

Making the mutual decision to stay healthy can help you feel connected to your partner. So rather than look at safe sex as an intimacy blocker, think of it as a responsible way to bond with someone. Be vulnerable; embrace the feelings of awkwardness that safer sex can trigger. She'll most likely find your realness to be a turn-on.

Nine

Ouch! That Feels Good:
Sensation Play for Rug Munchers

Playing with sensation and power dynamics doesn't require that you go out and spend a lot of money on leather outfits. And you don't have to attend any Renaissance Fairs or join secret clubs. It doesn't make you freaky (well, OK, it does, but in a good way) and it doesn't mean you are into pain or suffering from childhood trauma.

Things like bondage, domination, and submission bring a charged sense of sexual power to your bed that can be pretty exciting. And barking a few orders at your sweetheart ("Don't you dare move until I tell you to!") is a great way to break out of the same ol', same ol' rut.

Pussy-licking lends itself well to power games. You can "force" someone to go down on you. You can hold him down and fuck his face with your twat. You can pull her labia apart and expose her cunt before licking her, to make her feel vulnerable. You can tie your girl spread-eagle to the bed and lick her until she screams for you to stop. Or, my personal favorite, you can handcuff her and make her beg for it.

You may have experimented with domination and role play already. For example, holding your partner down during sex or telling them not to move while you go down on them are great ways to incorporate a little power into your oral sesh. If you'd like to take that thrill a little further, talk about it with your partner. Come up with a plan before you head off to Home Depot for dungeon supplies.

Can't afford a fully equipped playroom? Pick up some rope and eyebolts at the hardware store. Screw the eyebolts into the head and foot of your wooden futon frame—then tie your sweetie's hands and feet with soft nylon rope and secure the rope to the eyebolts. Voilà! Instant bondage bed!

The most important thing two people need when they want to get freaky is communication. You need to know what she wants. Does she want to be held down? She needs to know what you want. Do you want her to call you Officer? Figure it out. You don't have to hold a relationship conference or write each other letters, but something as simple as sitting down in a McDonald's and saying, "You know, honey, I really love it when you push my face into the pillow" will get the party started. If you want to try a little dominant/submissive role play action with your partner during sex, you'll first need to figure out which one of you wants which role. And you don't have to play the same role every time. Switching from one time to the next keeps things interesting. Try it.

It's a good idea to talk to your partner about your desire to dominate before you break out with the "Suck my clit now, you groveling little worm!" Also, once you've discussed the idea and you know which one of you wants to be boss and which one wants to be the secretary, you should stick with the same role for the entire evening's activities. Switching midway is sure to cause hurt feelings, not to mention confusion.

••

Bondage Safety!

Under no circumstances should you ever attach rope to anyone's neck. Don't tie anything tightly over any major arteries (i.e., pulse points like wrists, ankles, elbows, knees, armpits). Restraints should always be loose enough to slip a finger between the bottom's limb and the restraint. Use simple square knots that are easy to untie. Fancy knots and suspension bondage are only for serious BDSM players who know exactly what they are doing. Tops should check in with bottoms often.

••

Unsure whether you'd rather be top or bottom?
Take this quiz:

1. Handing out spankings turns me on.
   a. true
   b. false

2. I like to call the shots in bed.
   a. true
   b. false

3. I enjoy it when my lover says "please."
    a. true
    b. false

4. Turning my lover on excites me.
    a. true
    b. false

5. I want to be obeyed.
    a. true
    b. false

If you answered "a. true" to three or more questions, chances are good you'll enjoy being the top.

And now for the bottom quiz:

1. I like being bossed around in bed.
    a. true
    b. false

2. Being forced to perform sexually is exciting.
    a. true
    b. false

3. I fantasize about being tied up.
    a. true
    b. false

4. I enjoy being spanked.
    a. true
    b. false

5. Pain during sex is arousing.
   a. true
   b. false

Did you answer "a. true" to three or more questions? You probably want to be the bottom—you little slut, you.

Eight Things You Can Do to Please Your Bottom

- **Tie him or her up.** Use rope or restraints. Don't use scarves or anything that can tighten so much that they become difficult to remove without scissors. Also, play carefully with handcuffs; they can hurt.
- **Blindfold her.** Being blindfolded makes a bottom feel deliciously vulnerable.
- **Order her around.** Tell her what to do and how to do it. Practice saying "Lick me now" until it rolls off your tongue gracefully.
- **Put something in his or her mouth.** Underwear makes a nice gag.
- **Demand that she lie perfectly still while you tease her pussy with your tongue.**
- **Order him to stick out his tongue.** Then grind your pussy against his face.
- **"Force" her to watch you masturbate.**
- **Lick her puss,** but deny her orgasm until she pleads for it.

Ten Things You Can Do to Please Your Top

- **Worship her pussy with your tongue**—keep your hands behind your back for added excitement.
- **Lick her boots.**

- Call her "ma'am" or "sir."
- Display yourself in a lewd manner for her pleasure.
- Masturbate for her (only if she says you can!)
- Ask permission before coming.
- Beg for release.
- Promise her extravagant sexual favors.
- Bathe her.

Pump Up the Volume

Clit pumping is a neat trick for temporarily increasing the size of the clitoris. Female-to-male transfolk have been doing it forever. While this little trick lends itself well to gender-bending, you don't have to be male-gendered to want a larger, swollen, more sensitive clit. It's not for everybody, but those who get into it find the visual thrill as well as the added sensitivity to be pretty damn exciting.

You've probably seen penis pumps—big glass or acrylic cylinders with pumps attached that are designed to temporarily increase the size of a man's erection. Well, clit pumps are along the same lines, just smaller. Some manufacturers make pumps designed specifically for clits, or you can use a cylinder designed for nipple pumping; they are pretty much the same thing.

Pumps are available at most sex-toy stores, and some pumps designed specifically for clits have vibrators attached and other fun sex-gadget modifications.

Pumping works better if the pumpee is shaved. It's important to be able to create an airtight seal between the cylinder and her skin. Hair can get under the cylinder and break the seal. Lube her up well with something thick and tasteless. Then place the pump on her clit in such a way that a seal is made at the base of her bud. Close the valve and squeeze the bulb, pumping some of the air out of the chamber. Check in with her and see how she likes it. If it feels good, give the bulb another squeeze. She's probably feeling an intense suction on her clit. And the clit has most likely grown in size. Give the bulb a few more squeezes, watching closely and paying attention to her reactions. The throbby, pulling feeling should be pleasurable. If it isn't, stop immediately and release the valve. You can leave the pump on for a few minutes if you want to. But if this is a new activity for you, no more than 10 minutes is a good rule. As soon as you release the pressure her clit will return to near-normal size. But it will stay somewhat swollen and extra-sensitive for up to an hour afterward. Enjoy the heightened sensation she's feeling—and her extra-large clit— by giving it a soft, sensuous tongue bath.

Pain and Pleasure

Yummy vanilla sex feels great, but sometimes we want our fun to hurt a little. It doesn't have to be terribly painful. The sharp tug of hair getting pulled or the smack of a hand on a bare ass can be enough to send us flying. Pain feels especially exciting on aroused genitals. And in fact, once all our sex chemicals are flowing around, pain can become as stimulating as pleasure. Clamps, slapping, and biting can all add a new dimension to pussy-licking. Find out if the woman you are going down on enjoys playing with pain before you try any of these tricks. And as always, communicate!

Cool Her Down

Not ready for pain of any kind but interested in adding a different sensation to your box-licking? Try popping a couple of sugar-free mints into your mouth. The cool, icy sensation adds a neat little thrill. Menthol cough drops work well for this trick, but sugarless mints of any kind will do—the stronger the better. Suck on them a bit to get them going, then pop 'em between your cheek and gum while you eat her out. The icy sensation in your mouth will quickly transfer to her clit. Blow on her tender bits for added sensation. This feels especially exciting on the butt hole.

Clamp Her

Mean little clamps can be bought at any good sex shop. Test them first on your finger or the back of your hand to avoid overly painful surprises. Clamps can be applied to her outer labia. You can put on one or two or try making neat rows up and down. They can also be applied to her inner labia or even to her clitoral hood. If she's sufficiently aroused and you've done a good job of getting her juices flowing, then a little pinching is going to feel very exciting. Clamps work by restricting blood flow to the tissue. They hurt when you first put them on, but they hurt a whole lot more when you take them off and blood flows back into the area. You can create interesting sensations by tapping on the clamps or tugging on them with your teeth while they are in place. To add extra intensity, time the clamp removal with her orgasm.

Smack Her

Little smacks delivered to her vulva between tongue strokes can also feel very nice. Some women can orgasm from a good rhythmic slapping of their vulva. Try licking her for some time and then alternating licks and slaps to her clit. You can spank her entire vulva with the flat of your hand or just spank her mons with the tips of your fingers. Another trick is to use one hand to pull her mons up to expose her clitoral hood while using the other hand to place delicate slaps on her clitoral shaft.

Mini rubber or latex floggers are available at most good sex-toy shops. Try the resource guide for suggestions. These provide a stingy, tingling sensation. Lick her until she's very aroused and then try smacking her in different places on her vulva and see which spot elicits the best response.

Erotic Spanking

Spanking is a great precursor to oral sex. Actually, I think spanking is a great precursor to everything. Spanking is one of my favorite foreplay activities; it's exciting, a little kinky, and very, very erotic when done well. Think of a good spanking as a way to warm up her tush before you cool it off with your tongue. Talk about it first. Find out if she's interested in being spanked. This is not an activity to force on someone.

Also, the goal here is not to hurt your partner, but to make her feel good. So use a light touch. Bend her over something, the couch, a chair, your lap. Find a position that feels exciting to both of you.

Enjoy the intimacy this activity offers both of you. She's bent over and feeling very vulnerable. You are behind her with a very nice view of her cunt and ass. Grab her hips and pull her close to you. Make her feel sexy and desirable. If she's not used to being in such a submissive position, talk her through it. Tell her how hot she is. Run your hands up and down her back and ass and enjoy the feel of her skin and shape of her body.

Warm Her Up

Start out slowly by rubbing her butt cheeks for a while before you start smacking. Rub across her ass and graze your fingers against her exposed vulva for extra little chills and thrills. Begin by lightly tapping and patting her, letting your strikes slowly build in intensity. Let her become accustomed to the feel of your hand smacking her ass. Let some of your light smacks fall across her exposed vulva. The more turned on she is, the better your smacks will feel. So give her a long erotic warm-up.

Find Her Special Spot

Find the spot on her ass that stimulates her entire genital region. My ex-lover had a way of smacking the underside of my ass cheeks and barely grazing my vulva. It sent vibrations across my cunt that made me go crazy with pleasure. She'd tap, tap, tap on my ass till I was all worked up and then zero in on that special spot until I begged her to lick my pussy and make me come. Once you've figured out where she likes your hand best, spank around that spot and tease her. Don't remain focused on it or she'll grow used to the sensation and it will lose its zing.

Use Your Hand Creatively

Your hand can create many different sensations. Try cupping it or hitting her with the flat of your palm. Smacks with your hand relaxed and fingers spread will sting more than a tight flat palm-only smack. Use just the tips of your fingers to smack her cunt.

The Sound of One Hand Spanking

Sound is an important part of the turn-on factor in spanking. The noise of a sharp *thwack!* will send tingles down her spine and yours too. Aim for the fleshier parts of her butt to get a good reverb going. Backs of thighs make a good sound too. If you prefer the sound to the sensation, try the "spanky" available at most good sex-toy retailers. It has an attached leather flap that smacks against the paddle part when you use it. The paddle doesn't sting, but the leather flap provides a good sharp *crack*.

Vary the Sensation

Pause occasionally while spanking her to deliver different sensations to her sensitive butt. Try lightly scratching her bright red cheeks or rubbing her with your palm. You can also blow on her, rub her with ice, or rub something soft and furry across her cheeks.

Use Toys

Paddles are great. There are all sorts of sexy paddles out there with which you can accessorize your spanking sessions. Sportsheets makes a line of paddles that leave imprints of words like *ouch* or *love* on her butt. And the Star Raiser paddle available at Toys in Babeland leaves a bright red star behind. Other options for fun spanking include wooden spoons, spatulas, hairbrushes, or a slipper. You may want to use a tool to prevent your hand from getting sore. Depending on how spank-loving your partner is, your hand may wear out before she does.

Stay Connected

Check in with your partner to make sure she's enjoying all the sensation. Pay attention to the noises she's making. She may moan, gasp, or even cry. If you aren't sure what her reactions mean, ask her. Don't let her zone out. Talk to her and keep her connected to the action.

Keep the Beat

Once you've gotten her warmed up, find a beat and stick to it. She's getting off on the rhythmic sensation, and you don't want to ruin the groove she's in. If you're smacking her in a way that involves her clit, she may be able to orgasm from this. Many women can come from being spanked, so treat this sexual activity like you'd treat any other: Warm her up and then keep it going at a good speed until she's done.

Cool Down

When you've reached a stopping point, ask her what she'd like next. You are probably both pretty turned on by now. She may want you to turn her over and eat her out, or maybe she's ready for a good hard fucking, or maybe just some cuddling and rest. Whatever it is, maintain your intimate connection by staying physically in touch. And communicate with her about her desires.

Ten
Resource Guide

Here are some places to learn more about sex and buy neat stuff.

Retail Stores

Come Again Erotic Emporium
353 E. 53rd St.
New York, NY 10022
(212) 308-9394

Come as You Are
701 Queen St. West
Toronto, Ontario, Canada M6J 1E6
(416) 504-7934
www.comeasyouare.com

Condomania
647 N. Poinsettia Pl.
Los Angeles, CA 90036
(323) 930-5530
(800) 926-6366

351 Bleeker St.
New York, NY 10014
(212) 691-9442
www.condomania.com

Crimson Phoenix
1876 SW 5th Ave.
Portland, OR 07201
(503) 228-0129

Cupid's Treasure
3519 N. Halsted St.
Chicago, IL 60657
(773) 348-3884

Dream Dresser
8444-50 Santa Monica Blvd.
West Hollywood, CA 90069
(323) 848-3480
(800) 963-7326

1042 Wisconsin Ave. N.W.
Washington, DC 20007
(202) 625-0373
www.dreamdresser.com

Eros Boutique
581A Tremont St.
Boston, MA 02118
www.erosboutique.com

Eve's Garden
119 W. 57th St., Suite 420
New York, NY 10019
(800) 848-3837
(212) 757-8651
www.evesgarden.com

Fantasy Unlimited
102 Pike St.
Seattle, WA 98101
(206) 682-0167

Fetish Boutique
108 North Loop Blvd.
Austin, TX 78751
(512) 453-8090

Fetishes Boutique
704 S. Fifth St.
Philadelphia, PA 19147
(877) 2-CORSET
www.fetishesboutique.com

Forbidden Fruit
Body Art Salon
513 E. Sixth St.
Austin, TX 78751
(512) 476-4596

Toy Store and Education Center
512 Neches St.
Austin, TX 78701
(512) 478-8358
www.forbiddenfruit.com

Good For Her
175 Harbor St.
Toronto, Ontario, Canada M5S 1H3
(416) 588-0900
(877) 588-0900
www.goodforher.com

Good Vibrations
1210 Valencia St.
San Francisco, CA 94110
(415) 974-8980

1620 Polk St.
San Francisco, CA 94109
(415) 974-8985

2504 San Pablo Ave.
Berkeley, CA 94702
(510) 841-8987

Mail order (800) 289-8423
www.goodvibes.com

Grand Opening!
318 Harvard St., Suite 32
Arcade Bldg., Coolidge Corner
Brookline, MA 02446

8442 Santa Monica Blvd.
West Hollywood, CA 90069
(323) 848-6970

Toll-free ordering (877) 731-2626
(617) 731-2626
www.grandopening.com

Intimacies
28 Center St.
Northampton, MA 01060
(413) 582-0709
www.intimaciesonline.com

It's My Pleasure
4258 S.E. Hawthorne Blvd.
Portland, OR 97215
(503) 236-0505

Lovecraft
27 Yorkville Ave.
Toronto, Ontario, Canada M5R 1B7
(416) 923-7331
(877) 923-7331

2200 Dundas St. East
Mississauga, Ontario, Canada, L4X 2V3
(905) 276-5772
www.lovecraftsexshop.com

Passion Flower
4 Yosemite Ave.
Oakland, CA 94611
(510) 601-7750

Pleasure Chest
7733 Santa Monica Blvd.
West Hollywood, CA 90046
(800) 75-DILDO
(323) 650-1022
www.thepleasurechest.com

Pleasure Palace
277 Dalhousie St.
Ottawa, Ontario, Canada K1N 7E5
(613) 789-7866

Pleasure Place
1710 Connecticut Ave. N.W.
Washington, DC 20009
www.pleasureplace.com

Purple Passion
242 W. 16th St.
New York, NY 10011
(212) 807-0486
www.purplepassion.com

Romantasy
2191 Market St.
San Francisco, CA 94114
(800) 922-2281
www.romantasy.com

Rubber Tree
4426 Burke Ave. North
Seattle, WA 98103
(206) 663-4750

Sh!
22 Coronet St.
London N1 UK
(0171) 613-5456

Sin
4426 Burke Ave. North
Seattle, WA 98103
(206) 663-4750

Spartacus Leathers
300 S.W. 12th St.
Portland, OR 97205
(503) 224-2604

The Stockroom
4649 1/2 Russell Ave.
Los Angeles, CA 90027
(213) 666-2121
(800) 755-TOYS
www.stockroom.com

Stormy Leather
1158 Howard St.
San Francisco, CA 94103
(415) 626-1672
(877) 975-5577
www.stormyleather.com

Toys in Babeland
711 E. Pike St.
Seattle, WA 98122
(206) 328-2914

94 Rivington St.
New York, NY 10002
(212) 375-1701
Mail Order (800) 685-9119
www.babeland.com

Venus Envy
1598 Barrington St.
Halifax, Nova Scotia, Canada B3J 1Z6
(902) 422-0004
www.venusenvy.ns.ca

A Woman's Touch
600 Williamson St.
Madison, WI 53703
(888) 621-8880
(608) 250-1928
www.a-womans-touch.com

Womyn's Ware
896 Commercial Drive
Vancouver, BC
Canada, U5L 3Y5
(888) WYM-WARE
(604) 254-2543
www.womynsware.com

Online Shopping
(See retail stores as well.)

Adam and Eve www.adameve.com
Adam and Gillian's Sensual Whips and Toys www.aswgt.com
Aslan Leather www.aslanleather.com
Blowfish www.blowfish.com
Betty Dodson Productions www.bettydodson.com

E-Sensuals www.tanta.com
Femme Productions (Candida Royalle) www.royalle.com
Glyde Dams www.sheerglydedams.com
Heartwood Whips of Passion www.hearttoodwhips.com
House O'Chicks and Vulva University www.houseochicks.com
Libida www.libida.com
Nice-N-Naughty www.nice-n-naughty.com
Safe Sense www.condoms.net
SIR Video Productions www.sirvideo.com
Vixen Creations www.vixencreations.com
Xandria www.xandria.com

Web Sites

www.allsexguide.com
AltSex • www.altsex.org
Alyson Books • www.alyson.com
www.bondage.com
Susie Bright • www.susiebright.com
Clean Sheets • www.cleansheets.com
Cleis Press • www.cleispress.com
Dyke Planet • www.dykeplanet.com
Dykesworld • www.dykesworld.de
Erotica Readers and Writers Association • www.erotica-readers.com
FeMiNa • www.femina.com
www.hercurve.com
House O'Chicks • www.houseochicks.com
Jane's Net • www.janesguide.com
Lesbian Sex Mafia • www.lesbiansexmafia.org
Lesbianation • www.lesbianation.com
Libido Magazine • www.libidomag.com
National Leather Association • www.nla-i.com
Nerve • www.nerve.com
Queer Net • www.queernet.org
Scarlet Letters • www.scarletletters.com e
Scarleteen • www.scarlateen.com

Sexuality Information and Education Council of the United States
(SIECUS) • www.siecus.org
Society for Human Sexuality • www.sexuality.org
Technodyke • www.technodyke.com
Tiny Nibbles • www.tinynibbles.com
Tristan Taormino's Web site • www.puckerup.com
Venus or Vixen? • www.venusorvixen.com e
Web by Women for Women •
www.io.com/~wwwomen/sexuality/index.html
The Womb • www.womb.wwdc.com/tunnels.html

Resource Hotlines

American Social Health Association
(800) 971-8500

Centers for Disease Control and Prevention National AIDS Hotline
(800) 342-AIDS
Spanish (800) 344-7432
Hearing impaired (800) 243-7889
www.cdcnac.com

Domestic Violence Hotline
(800) 799-SAFE

HIV/AIDS Teen Hotline
(800) 440-TEEN

Los Angeles Sex Education Resources
(213) 486-4421

National Herpes Hotline
(919) 361-8488

National STD Hotline
(800) 227-8922

Planned Parenthood
(800) 230-PLAN
www.ppfa.org

Rape Abuse and Incest National Network (RAINN)
(800) 656-HOPE

Safer Sex Page
www.safersex.org

San Francisco Sex Information
(877) 472-7374 toll-free
(415) 989-7374
www.sfsi.org

Seattle Sex Information
(206) 328-7711

Informational/Instructional Web Sites

Alternate Sources • www.alternate.com
Andrea Nemerson's site for human sexuality • www.sfbg.com/asc
Annie Sprinkle's Web site • www.gatesofheck.com
Body Electric School • www.bodyelectric.org
Charles Haynes's Radical Sex • www.fifth-mountain.com/radical_sex
Coalition for Positive Sexuality (CPS) • www.positive.org
Columbia University information site • www.goaskalice.columbia.edu
Condomania information site • www.comdomania.com
Dr. Ruth • www.drruth.com
Federation of Feminist Women's Health Centers •
    www.fwhc.org
www.gayhealth.com
Gloria G. Brame's S/M site • www.gloria-brame.com
Human Awareness Institute • www.hai.org
IASHS Sexology NetLine • www.netaccess.on.ca/~sexorg/index.org
InstaTek Human Sexuality Site • www.instatek.com/sex/start.html

Masturbation site • www.jackinworld.com
Dr. Patti Briton • www.yoursexcoach.com
Queer Resources Directory • www.qrd.org
Safer Sex Resource • www.safersex.org
Sexual Health InfoCenter •
    www.sexhealth.org/infocenter/infomain.html
Sexual Health Network • www.sexualhealth.com
The Sex Institute • www.sexquest.com
Society for Human Sexuality •
    www.weber.u.washington.edu/~sfpse

Educational Videos/DVDS

The Amazing G-Spot and Female Ejaculation
    (Access International, 1999)
Bend Over Boyfriend (Fatale, 1998)
*Carol Queen's Great Vibrations: An Explicit Consumer Guide to
    Vibrations* (Blank Tapes Productions, 1995)
Faces of Ecstasy (Blank Tapes Productions, 1995)
Fire in the Valley: An Intimate Guide to Female Genital Massage
    (Sprinkle/Joseph Kramer, 1999)
How to Female Ejaculate (Fatale Video, 1992)
*How to Female Ejaculate; Find Your G-spot With Deborah
Sundahl* (Isis Media, 2002)
The Magic of Female Ejaculation (House O'Chicks, 1992)
Nice Girls... Films by and About Women (#11 Nice Girls Do It Nice)
    (Picture Start Inc., 1989)
Nina Hartley's Guides... (Adam and Eve Productions, 1994, 1996,
    2000) *to Anal Sex, Cunnilingus, Making Love to a Woman*
Private Pleasure and Shadows (Fatale Video, 1995)
Selfloving (Betty Dodson, 1991)
Sluts and Goddesses (Beatty/Sprinkle, 1992)
Ultimate Guide to Anal Sex for Women (Tristan Taormino, 1999)
Viva la Vulva: Women's Sex Organs Revealed
    (Betty Dodson, 1998)
Whipsmart (Good Vibrations' Sex Positive Productions, 2002)

Erotic Videos

The Black Glove (Bleu Visions, 1996)
Burlezk Live (Fatale Videos)
Dress Up for Daddy (Fatale Videos)
Hard Love (SIR Productions)
How to Fuck in High Heels (SIR Productions)
Hungry Hearts (Fatale Videos)
Leda and the Swan: Nailed (Bleu Visions, 1999)
Please Don't Stop (Good Vibrations' Sex Positive Productions, 2001)
Slide Bi Me (Good Vibrations' Sex Positive Productions, 2001)
Voluptuous Vixens (Good Vibrations' Sex Positive Productions, 2002)

Books

After Child Sexual Abuse, Stacie Haines (Cleis Press, 1999)
Anal Pleasure and Health: A Guide for Men and Women,
    Jack Morin (Down There Press, 1998)
Best American Erotica series, edited by Susie Bright (Simon & Schuster)
Best Lesbian Erotica series, edited by Tristan Taormino (Cleis Press)
Big, Big Love, Hanne Blank (Greenery Press, 1999)
Body Alchemy: Transsexual Portraits, Loren Cameron
    (Cleis Press, 1996)
*Can't Touch My Soul: A Guide for Lesbian Survivors of Child
    Sexual Abuse, Donna Rafanello (Alyson Books, 2004)*
The Clitoral Truth, Rebecca Chalker (Seven Stories Press, 2000)
Cunt: A Declaration of Independence, Inga Muscio
    (Seal Press, 1998)
Cunt Coloring Book, Tee Corinne (Naiad Press, 1989)
*Doing It for Daddy: Short Sexy Fiction About a Very Forbidden
    Fantasy,* edited by Pat Califia (Alyson Books, 1994)
*Enabling Romance: A Guide to Love, Sex and Relationships for the
    Disabled,* Ken Kroll and Erica Levy Klein (No Limits Communications,
    2001)
The Ethical Slut, Dossie Easton and Catherine Liszt
    (Greenery Press, 1997)
Female Masculinity, Judith Halberstam (Duke University Press, 1998)

Femme: Feminists, Lesbians, and Bad Girls, edited by Laura Harris
and Elizabeth Crocker (Routledge, 1997)
The Femme's Guide to the Universe, Shar Rednour
(Alyson Publications, 2000)
FTM: Female-to-Male Transsexuals in Society, Holly Devor
(Indiana University Press, 1997)
Gender Outlaw, Kate Bornstein (Vintage Books, 1994)
The Good Vibrations Guide to the G-Spot, Cathy Winks
(Down There Press, 1998)
The Good Vibrations Guide to Sex, Third Edition, Cathy Winks and
Anne Semans (Cleis Press, 2002)
A Hand in the Bush: The Art of Vaginal Fisting, Deborah Addington
(Greenery Press, 1998)
Health Care Without Shame, Charles Moser Ph.D., M.D. (Greenery
Press, 1999)
Herotica Series, Vol. 1-7, various editors (Penguin/Plume)
Leatherfolk: Radical Sex, People, Politics and Practice, edited
by Mark Thompson (Alyson Books, 2001)
The Lesbian Sex Book, Second Edition, Wendy Caster,
revised by Rachel Kramer Bussel (Alyson Books, 2003)
New View of a Woman's Body, Federation of Feminist Women's
Health Centers (Feminist Health Press, 1991)
On Our Backs: The Best Erotic Fiction, edited by Lindsay McClune
(Alyson Books, 2001)
On Our Backs: The Best Erotic Fiction, Volume 2, edited by
Diana Cage (Alyson Books, 2004)
The On Our Backs Guide to Lesbian Sex, edited by Diana Cage
(Alyson Books, 2004)
Our Bodies, Ourselves for the New Century, Boston Women's
Health Collective (Simon & Schuster, 1998)
Public Sex: The Culture of Radical Sex, Pat Califia (Cleis Press, 1994)
Real Live Nude Girl Carol Queen (Cleis Press, 2002)
Sensuous Magic: A Guide for Adventurous Couples, Patrick Califia
(Cleis Press, 2001)
Sex Changes: The Politics of Transgenderism, Patrick Califia
(Cleis Press, 2002)
Sex for One: The Joy of Selfloving, Betty Dodson
(Crown Publishers/Harmony Press, 1987)

Speaking in Whispers: Lesbian African-American Erotica, edited by
    Kathleen E. Morris (Third Side Press, 1996)
The Strap-on Book, A.H. Dion (Greenery Press, 1999)
Susie Bright's Sexwise, Susie Bright (Cleis Press, 1995)
Susie Sexpert's Lesbian Sex World, Susie Bright
    (Cleis Press, 1990, 1998)
*Transgender Warrior: Making History from Joan of Arc to Dennis
    Rodman,* Leslie Feinberg (Beacon, 1997)
Trans Liberation, Leslie Feinberg (Beacon, 1998)
Transmen and FTMs: Identities, Bodies, Genders and Sexualities,
    Jason Cromwell (University of Illinois Press, 1999)
The Ultimate Guide to Anal Sex for Women, Tristan Taormino
    (Cleis Press, 1997)
The Ultimate Guide to Cunnilingus, Violet Blue (Cleis Press, 2002)
The Ultimate Guide to Strap-On Sex, Karlyn Lotney
    (Cleis Press, 2000)
The Whole Lesbian Sex Book: A Passionate Guide for All of Us,
    Felice Newman (Cleis Press, 1999)

About the Author

Diana Cage is the editor of *On Our Backs* magazine, a national lesbian sex magazine. She also edited *On Our Backs Guide to Lesbian Sex* and *On Our Backs: The Best Erotic Fiction Volume Two* as well as the anthology *Bottoms Up: Writing About Sex*. Diana is a contributing writer for *Girlfriends* magazine, and her fiction and nonfiction are widely published in anthologies and journals, most recently in *From Porn to Poetry 2, Up All Night, Leaving Her, Blithe House Quarterly, Kitchen Sink, Clean Sheets,* and *Eros Guide.* She lives in San Francisco.